St. GERARDINE Pr.

LOSSIEMOUTH.

Every Child's Book of
BIRDS AND
BIRD-WATCHING

Every Child's Book of

BIRDS AND

BIRD-WATCHING

HENRY MAKOWSKI
Translated by KATHLEEN SHAW

Edited and adapted by JOHN SEYMOUR

 LONDON & TORONTO

ACKNOWLEDGEMENTS

The publishers wish to thank Eric Hosking and all those who supplied illustrations for the original German edition of this book. Figure 63 is reproduced by kind permission of George Newnes Ltd., from the book *Down the Long Wind* by Garth Christian. The frontispiece is from a photograph of a tawny owl by Ardea Photographics.

The jacket illustration is reproduced from a photograph of Gannets taken by R. W. Kennedy

The publishers also wish to acknowledge the kind assistance readily given in the selection of illustrations for this edition by the late John Markham.

ISBN 0 222 00176 3

Burke Publishing Company Limited
14 John Street, London, WC1N 2EJ
Burke Publishing (Canada) Limited
73 Six Point Road, Toronto 18, Ontario
Printed in Great Britain by
T. and A. Constable Ltd., Edinburgh

Contents

CHAPTER ONE

Who Watches Birds and Why

International enthusiasm for ornithology · The amateur and the scientist co-operate · Birds through the ages · A modern hobby

ENTHUSIASM FOR BIRDS is now widespread and during this century bird-watching has become a popular hobby. The British are not alone in this, and already there are thousands of bird-watchers in America, Europe and Russia.

At each change of the seasons, millions of birds set out on migration. They travel long distances, often migrating through several countries and, in some cases, from continent to continent. There is nothing unusual in the fact that birds fly from one side of the Iron Curtain to the other, but it is indeed remarkable that people of different political creeds should be eager to exchange information on any subject. Birds have a way of arousing tremendous interest, and ornithology —the study of birds—is truly international. Bird-watchers in one country cannot bear to be left in ignorance about where birds go after they have flown away, and people want to compare notes on how birds behave in various countries.

The study of birds attracts people of all ages and from all walks of life. Originally it was confined mainly to people of leisure who lived in the country but the enthusiasm has spread in a remarkable way to people living in cities and towns. It is sometimes said, for instance, that more is known about birds of the London area than about those of any other part of the British Isles.

It is true that the gulf between Man and Nature appears to have widened with the expansion of built-up areas. Only one hundred years ago the majority of people still lived in the country or in small towns, where woods, meadows and open countryside were close at hand. Now people are attracted to the large cities with their opportunities for well-paid work and their many forms of entertainment. Although Man now lives in artificial surroundings where the rhythm of the seasons and the starkness of Nature are softened and cushioned by the comforts of civilization,

This black-headed gull might well spend the winter in a built-up area

he is still attracted by any form of wild life. Birds still find a living in the cities and in some cases their numbers have increased. For instance, black-headed gulls have now largely left the coast and thousands of them haunt the inland, built-up areas in winter. The way in which birds adapt themselves to living alongside Man is one of many branches of ornithology which absorbs the interest of amateurs and professionals alike.

It may seem strange that, in this age of science and technology, there should be any subject left in which amateur and scientist can work together, side by side, with each contributing to the knowledge and enjoyment of the other. It so happens that ornithology combines two aspects: firstly, work in the field, observing birds in their natural surroundings; and secondly, work in the laboratory and reference library, interpreting the results of field observations with the aid of scientific method. It is in field-work that the keen and energetic young bird-watcher often excels.

Bird-watching is not a comfortable hobby. It drives you out of doors in all kinds of weather while your friends enjoy the comfort of sitting by the fire and eating meals at normal hours; it makes you walk miles over rough ground, it keeps you rooted to one spot in uncomfortable positions, it gets you up before dawn and keeps you out all through the night. One must be prepared to face jokes and jibes from friends and suspicious accusations from policemen and respectable citizens. In short, it is not a hobby for the unadventurous. But it is a hobby which lasts a lifetime and which brings you into contact with all kinds of people. If you take up bird-watching, you will never feel bored or dull again.

Birds attract us from a very early age and we are all familiar with nursery rhymes such as *Who Killed Cock Robin?* Fairy stories, traditional tales and legends provide ample proof of our interest in birds. Although bird-watching as we know it today is a modern development, the record of Man's close association with birds stretches back as far as the history of Man himself.

Birds through the ages

Cave paintings and ancient sculptures provide evidence that birds were regarded by prehistoric Man as sufficiently important to merit portrayal in lasting memorials. For instance, a bas-relief sculpture found in the ruins of Khorsabad (Iraq) was described by Sir A. H. Layard (the excavator of Nineveh) as showing "a falconer bearing a hawk on his wrist". This suggests that falconry was known some 700 years before Christ in Assyria.

The famous prehistoric caves at Lascaux in France were discovered in 1940 by four schoolboys who were taking their dog for a walk in the Dordogne district. The dog fell down a hole in the ground which had been left by the uprooting of a tree; when the boys investigated the hole, they found that it led to a network of caves. On the cave walls were paintings which had probably not been seen for 20,000 to 30,000 years. One of the paintings shows a man lying on his back near a wounded bison; the man is wearing a birdlike mask and below him is a long-legged bird with no feet.

The fact that the bird was painted

FIGURE I *Cave painting at Lascaux—note the bird (without feet) in the foreground*

The golden eagle

with no feet may seem curious but we find, much later on in history, birds still being used as symbols, and again without feet. In heraldry, for instance, one of the common bird devices is the martlet: a small bird depicted without feet. Birds were often used as heraldic devices on armorial bearings. Historical records include the following examples: In the fourteenth century there was John Pyehale who sealed with arms of "three magpies". Then there was Naunton who bore "sable, three martlets silver" and Heron who bore "azure, three herons silver". Eagles are also prominent in heraldry, possibly a development from the days when Roman legionaries carried a standard surmounted by an eagle.

Birds have been used by Man for sport as well as for symbolism from the earliest times. Pliny and Aristotle refer to falconry in Europe and ancient Persian and Arabic manu-

The kestrel; in the Middle Ages it was a knave's hawk

scripts have also been found to contain references to falconry. It was not, however, until the Middle Ages that falconry became a popular sport in Britain. Certain kinds of birds then became identified with certain classes of people and the kind of hawk which you carried was an indication of your status. For instance, a peregrine was associated with an earl, a goshawk

FIGURE 2 *The goshawk, at one time used in falconry*

with a yeoman, a kestrel with a knave and a sparrow-hawk with a "holy water clerk", while a merlin was a lady's hawk.

Falconry has now declined in popularity; most people are more strongly attracted by the excitement of seeing birds of prey under completely wild conditions. For many bird-watchers, sighting a peregrine or eagle is a rare and thrilling experience.

A modern hobby

Each year in America there is a Christmas bird count on 26th December. Amateurs and professionals set out in the early hours of the morning and the great count is on. One group of observers in Florida travelled 10,000 miles and spent a total of 500 hours observing and counting birds; on this occasion they listed 78,000 birds.

In Britain there are regular counts of wildfowl throughout the winter months. From September to March about eight hundred people turn out on the same Sunday each month to count wildfowl all over Britain. These counts are organized by the Wildfowl Trust from its headquarters at Slimbridge in Gloucestershire where Peter Scott (the famous artist and ornithologist) has assembled a remarkable collection of wildfowl from all over the world.

Bird-watching today is a hobby supported by a modern network of societies and organizations. There are local natural history societies which arrange lectures, film shows and field outings. There are Field Study Centres and Bird Observatories where young people can attend residential courses, combining theoretical and practical work. Some information on these

The pintail, one of the birds covered by the counts organized by the Wildfowl Trust

The eider duck which can be seen at the Wildfowl Trust

activities is given at the end of this book. Fuller details are available from The Council for Nature, Zoological Gardens, Regents Park, London NW1 4RY.

There are two main societies in Britain which are entirely devoted to birds. The Royal Society for the Protection of Birds is a national body which is responsible for the protection of birds; it owns and manages a number of Nature Reserves and it aims at educating both adults and children. The British Trust for Ornithology promotes research into all branches of ornithology and organizes permanent studies such as the Nest Records Scheme and Bird-ringing.

Books and publications about birds are now so numerous that it is difficult to appreciate our luck in having so much of other people's knowledge put at our disposal today. Before this century books about birds were few and far between. It was during the sixteenth century that possibly the earliest known bird book was published. Conrad Gesner, a famous Swiss naturalist, wrote and compiled a set of twenty-one volumes of natural history books, including one about birds. Some of Gesner's material came from mediæval bestiaries and from works which had been written as long ago as in the days of the Ancient Greeks and Romans.

Returning to more modern times, a bird book which is still regarded as a classic was published in 1789. This is Gilbert White's *Natural History of Selborne*. Before White's time chiff-chaffs, willow warblers and wood warblers were all thought to be the same kind of bird. Gilbert White was the first person to notice that, although they looked similar, they had different songs. His book is a masterpiece of how to observe Nature and every bird-watcher should be familiar with it.

Coming right up to date, there are many excellent books on birds, but it is generally accepted that the standard work of reference for Britain is Witherby's *Handbook of British Birds*. It consists of five volumes. These are unfortunately now out of print; young bird-watchers may have to be content with borrowing it from the shelves of the local library. A number of less technical books are listed in the Appendix.

Now that you know something about the people who watch birds and the kind of help you can get in finding out about birds, you will want to get on with some bird-watching. It is possible to watch birds and yet notice nothing in particular. How much do you really know about birds? Although you may have

listened to bird song, do you know *why* birds sing? Perhaps you have watched a large bird landing carefully on a swaying branch, do you know *how* it manages to perch safely without overbalancing? Do all birds migrate? Do you know how they find their way on their long journeys?

Some knowledge of these things will help you to watch birds intelligently. It is much more exciting if you know what to look for and how to interpret what you see, and it is well worth taking the trouble to learn something about the fundamentals of bird life.

The willow warbler, which Gilbert White christened "the middle willow wren"

CHAPTER TWO

The Sounds Birds Make

*Bird song and bird calls · Recordings and their
use in agriculture and aviation · Identification*

WHY DO BIRDS SING? Does a bird sing for its own pleasure? Does it sing in order to help pass the time for its mate on the nest? Or, is it for some other reason altogether?

Bird song has three main functions: firstly, to indicate the boundaries of the bird's territory; secondly, to attract a mate; and thirdly, to intimidate rivals. These three functions overlap and intermingle; by observing the detailed circumstances in which a bird sings, you can learn a lot about the way birds live.

A bird's territory is governed by the position of the site on which the nest will be built. The site must be suitable not only for building the nest but also for rearing the young birds, preferably safe from enemies and within easy reach of a supply of food.

Supposing a starling has selected a certain nestbox in a garden or wood; it sits by the nestbox, fluttering its wings and singing loudly. When a second starling appears it sings even louder, and as the second starling approaches, our first starling dives on the intruder; this is a sign that the intruder is a male (cock) which must be driven away. A little later a third starling comes into the territory, again the volume of song increases but this time the intruder is not intimidated and slips quietly into the nestbox; this is a sure sign that the intruder is a female (hen) and is a potential mate.

Put into words the song starts: *This is my home.* When the rival cock approaches it continues: *Keep away, this is mine.* Finally, there follows an aggressive *Get out!* As the hen bird is recognized, the song becomes a courtship phrase, such as: *Come and be mine, in the home I have chosen.*

You often see blackbirds chasing each other around and singing loudly at the same time. A cock blackbird with bright orange beak is a fine sight as it proclaims its territory, singing often from the same perch or "song post". One bird may have several song posts, and by noticing where these are you can get a rough idea of the extent of the territory.

The blackbird. He often sings from the same "song post"

Territorial boundaries are invisible but it is possible to find out where they lie. If one puts a model bird close to a branch on which a wild bird of the same species is singing, the wild bird will swoop down on its model rival; as the model bird is moved away from the centre of the wild bird's territory, the attacks get less ferocious and when they stop completely, the invisible boundary has been crossed.

Bird song

Knowledge of bird song can be useful in estimating how many pairs of birds are living in a given area. By counting all the singing cocks, the bird population can be estimated. To do this, of course, it is essential to be familiar with the song of every species of bird in the area. There are no hard-and-fast rules about how to

FIGURE 3 *The approximate musical score of a blackbird's song*

memorize bird song, there are no easy short cuts and it requires a great deal of patient listening.

16

Some people find it easiest to make up words which seem to fit each phrase, such as: *A little bit of bread and no cheese* for the yellowhammer. Other people find it easier to compare each song phrase with a musical tune. Many composers are said to have made use of bird song in their works. Richard Strauss begins the first act of his opera *Der Rosenkavalier* with a melody of a blackbird. Maurice Ravel is said to have composed a rather melancholy arabesque for the piano after listening to birds singing in a dark wood at Fontainebleau.

Even if you are musical, it is not easy to notate bird song because most of the notes produced by birds are not quite pure. It is best to forget music and concentrate on the pattern of the rise and fall of notes and the rhythm of each phrase.

The long winter months do not give much opportunity for studying

The yellowhammer at the nest with her young. The song of her mate seems to say "A little bit of bread and no cheese"

17

bird song in the field because there are so few birds singing, but it is an excellent time of year to learn to identify songs at home, by listening to recordings which are now available on commercial disks. The largest collection of recordings appears in Witherby's *Sound-Guide to British Birds*, by Myles North and Eric Simms; it

Bird calls

Birds use their voices not only for singing but for making a variety of calls which are heard by other birds which react accordingly. If you listen to a flock of jackdaws in a field, you will be able to distinguish two definite calls among the chatter; as long as the birds feel safe, they make a sound

FIGURE 4 *The jackdaw, whose call keeps the flock in touch*

FIGURE 5 *This is a jay. Birds give alarm calls when jays are about because jays eat eggs*

contains songs and calls of 195 species. This could be rather a bewildering variety for some people, but there are many records that feature fewer birds and may be more suitable for beginners. On some of the records the birds' names are announced; in other cases the calls are only identified in an accompanying leaflet. If he wishes to, the listener can test his knowledge by covering the leaflet up. A selection of records are listed in the Appendix; although rather expensive, they are far better at describing bird calls than books, which can only use words like "tsip" and "haark"!

like *Caw, caw*, but as soon as danger threatens their voices take on a different note and they are up and away with a great flurry of wings. Birds which move about in flocks often make calls which keep the members of the flock in contact with each other.

Winter may be a poor time for hearing bird *song* in the field but it is an excellent time for becoming familiar with the warning and alarm *calls* made by various species. The trees are bare, birds can readily see their enemies and also be seen by them. Alarm calls are warnings of danger, and all sound rather alike. Birds have different songs but when an enemy is about they all "speak the same language" and so manage to warn one another.

Every kind of bird has a number of calls. They can only be recognised with practice and it will take many field excursions to learn even a

and poisoning were of little use in fighting this menace. Then someone had the idea of recording the warning cry of a rook, to play back to the birds in the fields. It took many recordings to single out the right call, but at last all these efforts were rewarded and as soon as the rooks heard these calls they took off in

FIGURE 6 *The scarecrow is sometimes replaced today by recorded alarm calls*

FIGURE 7 *Rooks like this one come to each other's aid*

limited number. Sooner or later you will be taken in by a starling, for starlings are masters of deception and they can imitate almost any other bird call or sound that they have heard.

The study of birds' voices has proved to be of great economic value in agriculture. In northern France, for example, rooks cause a lot of damage to crops every year. In some districts certain crops, such as maize, can hardly be grown because large flocks of rooks descend and eat the seeds almost as soon as they are put into the ground. Scarecrows, shooting

confusion. Some of them even flew towards the loudspeaker van as though to come to the aid of the bird in distress.

Similar methods have been used in the fight against starlings in areas where cherries and grapes are grown commercially. There remains only one question: How long will it be before the birds get used to the recordings and resume their plundering? Time will tell whether this method of scaring away birds is of lasting usefulness.

Airport authorities and pilots are also interested in these experiments;

one often hears of the damage that birds can do to an aircraft, sometimes resulting in loss of life. In Holland, hundreds of gulls used to rest on the heated runways during cold weather; the airport authorities appealed to ornithologists for advice. Once again recordings were used, this time of a gull's alarm call, and loudspeakers transmitted the warning cry just before each plane took off, clearing the runway in a very short time.

So far, we have concentrated on learning and memorizing the sounds birds make but we have not mentioned how the birds which make these sounds should be identified and named. There is so much to learn all at once when you start. Studying birds is not a hobby for the person who wants to take life easily: it demands patience, concentration and a sense of curiosity about the ways in which birds live. Identifying birds by

Woodlarks, whose song was the source of Ravel's inspiration for one of his piano works

Lapwings like this one often menace the safety of airport runways as do winter flocks of gulls

their appearance should go hand-in-hand with memorizing their songs and calls. Winter is a good time to start because fewer species are making sounds and, without leaves on the trees, you have a better chance of seeing the birds in detail. The more you can learn in the winter, the more ready and prepared you will be for the great influx of spring migrants. Once spring and summer arrive, you will want to be out in the field at every available minute of the day. Winter is the time, therefore, for studying books and gaining theoretical knowledge about such things as the physical structure of a bird, how it keeps warm and how it flies.

21

CHAPTER THREE

Physical Structure and Classification

*Feathers and their uses · How does a bird perch? · Classifica-
tion and names of birds · Genus, species and sub-species*

BIRDS ARE VERTEBRATES. This is another way of saying that they have backbones. Their skeletons are built on much the same lines as any other backboned animal but they are better at flying than any other vertebrate (with the possible exception of bats). Why is it that birds can fly so well?

The whole body of a bird is geared to flight. Like an aircraft, it has a strong but light framework and its design is streamlined. Weight is reduced to a minimum as bones and feathers are hollow. Any irregularity or unevenness in bone structure is smoothed out by a covering of feathers so that the body offers as little resistance as possible to the wind.

Gliding is the simplest form of flight in which support is provided by currents of air. If you make a paper aeroplane and launch it, you can watch how the air supports the light frame. A bird glides in much the same way as a man-made glider, using its

pinions as wing-flaps while its tail feathers function as a rudder. Birds sometimes glide or soar for long periods and to do this they need up-currents. This uplift can be observed in gulls and birds of prey. Other species with different techniques gain height and uplift by creating air currents with wing flapping.

Feathers and their uses

The feathers which cover a bird's body not only give it a streamlined silhouette for flying, they also keep the bird warm. Birds are very active, they use a great deal of energy in flying; being warm-blooded their body temperature would drop rapidly without some form of insulation. Even the parts of the bird's body which are not covered by feathers are constructed in such a way that little heat is lost. The beak, for instance, is horny and the exposed part of the leg is covered with scaly skin. In extreme temperatures the blood-

vessels of the skin contract and it has been proved that in very hard weather birds die from lack of food rather than from the cold. Twelve to fourteen hours without food can easily mean death to tits · and one long cold winter's night may be the undoing of a large number of birds.

The feathers can be divided, broadly speaking, into two groups: large feathers which are used in flight and for manœuverability— mainly in wings and tail—and small feathers which afford a protective covering. Lying close to the body, the soft down provides a soft under-coat and the space between each feather helps insulation.

Have you ever looked at a feather under a microscope? Each single feather is a masterpiece of construction. The quill, or backbone, is elastic and has many small chambers. At opposite sides of the quill and pointing forwards are the barbs. Out of the barbs, again at a forward angle, grow the barbules. These barbules have tiny hooks on one side which lock on to neighbouring barbules. The whole structure is thus held together quite firmly without being rigid. In a bird's wing all the feathers overlap so that on the up-stroke they fan out, letting air pass through the gaps, and on the down-stroke they lie close together, giving

FIGURE 8 *A buzzard in flight*

added power to the wing. Birds have an astonishing number of feathers: a mute swan, for instance, has about 25,000 feathers, of which 80 per cent cover the neck.

How does a bird perch?

When you watch birds apparently balancing precariously on slender twigs, you may wonder why they do not fall off. The answer lies in the construction of a bird's foot. Perhaps at some time or other you have had

FIGURE 9 *An enlarged and diagrammatic view of a single feather*

23

The feet of this green woodpecker feeding its young are an ideal example of the way in which a bird's toes are always suited to its method of perching

is a cord called a tendon running down the bird's leg to its claws. When the bird perches, the weight of its body folds the legs, and the tendon pulls the claws tightly round the perch. So, even when a bird is asleep, it cannot fall off its perch.

Nearly all birds have four toes and the majority of perching birds have three toes pointing forward and one pointing backward. There are some exceptions: woodpeckers have two toes pointing forward and two pointing backward; owls and cuckoos can also position their toes in this way. The way in which a woodpecker uses its foot is particularly interesting: the second and third toe point forward, carrying the main weight of the body, the fourth toe spreads out sideways, gripping the side of the tree trunk in much the same way as an engineer uses climbing irons on a telegraph pole.

The construction of a bird's foot differs according to its way of life. Birds of prey have powerful feet and sharp talons with which to grasp their prey; divers have webbed feet for swimming and diving but waders, which spend much of their time walking on soft mud, are only partially webbed. You can often tell just by looking at a bird's feet what sort of life it leads: whether it is a percher, a swimmer, a climber, a wader and so on. Similarly a bird's beak varies according to its method of feeding.

a budgerigar perching on your finger; you can feel the claws gripping your finger as the weight of the body presses directly down on to its legs and feet. If you straighten the budgie's legs you can feel its claws relax. There

FIGURE 10 *The lesser spotted woodpecker— note the way it uses its feet*

FIGURE 12 *The woodcock*

Insect eaters have small pointed bills, waders have long slender bills for probing mud and seed eaters have short and stocky bills that are very strong.

The shapes of various parts of a bird offer definite clues as to how it spends its time. After a while you will begin to notice certain "family-likenesses" between groups of birds and you may even try guessing to which family they belong. When you reach this stage you are more than halfway to learning something about bird classification.

Classification and names

The original classification of birds

FIGURE 11 *The osprey*

was based upon "family-likenesses" and was made in the eighteenth century by a famous Swedish naturalist, Carl von Linné, usually known as Linnaeus. The Linnaean system is the foundation of our present classification but it has been developed and enlarged. It gives birds scientific names, in Latin, according to their classification.

When you look up a bird in a reference book you may be puzzled by the fact that each one has a name, in two or three parts, in Latin. You may be tempted to say that there is no need to learn scientific names when English names are so much easier to remember. The fact is that there are a number of birds

FIGURE 13 *An insect-eater, one of the warblers*

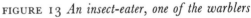

25

A nightjar flying over bracken and gorse at night

which are known by several names, often based on dialect and local tradition. A nightjar is sometimes called a goat-sucker or fern-owl, a lapwing is known as a peewit or green plover, a hedge-sparrow as a dunnock or dykie and so on. This variety of names, even in one language, is confusing but it becomes even more chaotic when several languages are involved. As Latin is accepted as the international language of science, it is obviously much easier to use the scientific name in exchanging information about a bird with people from other countries.

An additional advantage in learning scientific names arises from the fact that the name tells you quite a lot about the bird. The first Latin word tells you to which *genus* it belongs, the second word indicates the *species* and the third word may indicate a *sub-species or race*. To describe a species in a few words is difficult but it is a population of individuals which resemble each other, more or less closely, and which interbreed with each other rather than with somewhat similar populations inhabiting the same area. A sub-species is a population of a species inhabiting different geographical areas from other populations of the same species and differing in certain small details. The genus is a relatively large group whose members resemble each other in a general way; the species is a smaller group and the sub-species is the smallest unit of all.

This may sound rather confusing, but if you think in terms of a human family it may help. All the members of one family have a family likeness and are called by the same surname; each child differs from the others and has an individual first name. Now look at the crow family:

FIGURE 14 *The nightjar, also known as a goat-sucker*

Raven—*Corvus corax corax*
Carrion-crow—*Corvus corone corone*
Hooded crow—*Corvus corone cornix*
Rook—*Corvus frugilegus frugilegus*
Scandinavian jackdaw—*Corvus monedula monedula*
Jackdaw—*Corvus monedula spermalogus*

The first part of the scientific name in each case is *Corvus* which indicates the birds are members of the crow family (*Corvidae*). The second part indicates that they differ in detail and the third part indicates a difference such as that between the jackdaws.

Ornithologists are working all the time on classifying birds; opinions vary about whether certain birds should be classified as species, sub-species and so on. When you consider that there are around 8,600 birds already named in the world, of which 452 are found in Europe, it is hardly surprising that there should be differences of opinion. It is a complicated subject and need not concern the amateur in detail but it is well worth learning the main families so that you can be on the look-out for relationships between birds.

27

Bullfinch

Blue tit

Crested tit

Marsh tit

Hawfinch

Brambling

Greenfinch

Great tit

Tree sparrows

Yellowhammer

House sparrow

Sparrow-hawk

Barn owl

Great
spotted
woodpecker

Tawny owl

Nuthatch

Waxwing

Wren

Jay

W. Söllner

FIGURE 15 *These birds may all be seen in parts of Britain during the winter*

CHAPTER FOUR

How to Attract Birds to Your Garden

Making a bird table and a bird bath · Food for birds · The most frequent visitors

Having learned at least some of the fundamentals of bird life, the time has come to begin some practical work and the most convenient place to start is in your garden. The first step is to attract some of the local birds so that you can watch them at relatively close quarters and at frequent intervals. The easiest way to do this is to make a bird table and attract birds to it by putting out food and water.

Bird tables

A bird table will only serve its purpose well if it is made in such a way that birds can use it safely, without being in constant danger from cats. It should also protect the

food from wind and rain, and if possible the food should be out of reach of squirrels. You can quite easily make a bird table like the one in figure 22. It should be too tall for cats to jump on to and it should stand well away from overhanging branches so that squirrels cannot leap down from the trees and steal the food. Squirrels are good at climbing; to prevent them getting up the supporting pole, it is a good idea to include an obstacle that they cannot get past. This can be readily made from a large biscuit tin. The lid is not required. Make a hole in the bottom of the tin, turn the tin upside down, and then push the bird table pole through the hole. The tin should be about 4 ft. (120 cm.) above the ground, so that squirrels cannot jump straight on to it. Even with the tin installed, some squirrels might reach the table by taking a run at the pole and climbing it fast enough to be able

FIGURE 16 *This bird table is not very practical because the wind will blow the food away*

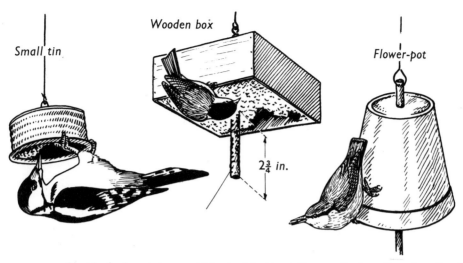

FIGURE 17 *Simple food containers which should attract the woodpecker, tit and nuthatch*

to scramble round the tin. They cannot do this, however, if the pole is smooth. The best protection of all is probably a length of plastic drain-pipe covering the pole.

The roof over the table is not essential, but it does help keep rain off both the food and the birds that are eating it. Low "walls" round the sides of the tray are also a good idea, as they prevent small pieces of food being blown away. There should be gaps in the walls at the corners of the tray so that any rainwater on the table can drain off.

Besides using a table, there are many other ways of putting out food. One of the simplest and quickest items to prepare is a flower-pot, suspended upside down. This makes

FIGURE 18 *Coconut and feeding-ring suspended out of reach of cats*

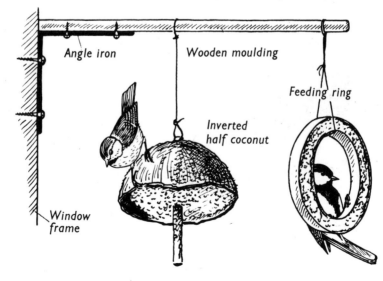

This great tit is tame enough to take food from a human being

a container for the type of food which tits like to eat. The pot should not be too large. Place a smooth stick through the hole; this will serve as a perch. The shorter end of this stick is used to suspend the pot and the longer end should project through the food for about 3 in. (7 cm.). A small nail driven through the stick before it is inserted in the pot will help to keep this in position. An empty coconut shell, or even a small tin with a hole punched in the bottom, will serve just as well as a flowerpot. You may prefer to use a cardboard ring already filled with fat and seeds, but whatever type of container you use, it has to be suspended somehow. To do this satisfactorily, you will need a lath about 12 in. (30 cm.) long and 1 in. by 1 in. (2½ cm. by 2½ cm.) thick; this is fastened to the wall or window frame by an angle bracket.

There are many other types of containers which can be made at practically no cost. The stalks of sunflowers can be used in the following way: cut a length of about 15 in. (33 cm.) of stalk, split this lengthwise so that about one-third of the stalk is removed, scrape out the pulp from the remaining piece except for 1½ in. (4 cm.) at either end of the

stalk—this gives you a narrow trough, and a notch or two at each end will help you to fix string or wire for holding the trough in place. Figure 19 shows several ways of fastening it to or suspending it from a tree—suspension is preferable where there are cats in the neighbourhood. (Bamboo will serve just as well as sunflower stems.)

What sort of food are you going to put in these containers? The easiest way of making sure that the food will not fall out is to use melted fat as a base and tip some seeds into this; the fat then cools and holds the seeds in position; it is just a question of trial and error in getting the right proportion of fat to seeds. Chopped biscuits, crumbled cake, nuts and bacon rinds cut into short lengths (so that birds do not choke on them) are also suitable. Do not put out too much fat or some of it will remain uneaten and go mouldy.

A popular container consists of a

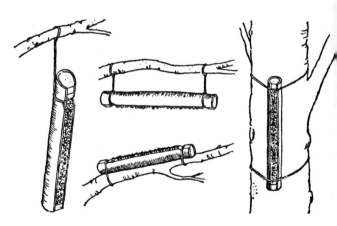

FIGURE 19 *Methods of attaching small feeding-troughs made from sunflower or bamboo stalks*

metal cage whose mesh is small enough to hold peanut kernels. These cages are quite cheap to buy from shops and various suppliers. They can be suspended from the branches of trees or from a bird table.

A number of birds, like hedge-sparrows, robins and chaffinches, prefer to feed on the ground; suitable food can be scattered on a lawn or path for them. Choose a place well out in the open, so that cats cannot approach without being seen in good time. Great spotted woodpeckers are among the birds attracted to pieces of cheese pressed into the bark of trees. A good way of offering lumps of fat is to hang them from a rope strung across part of the garden like a washing-line. Make a hole in each lump of fat and pass a piece of string through. Then tie the string to the rope. Fat attracts a number of birds including long-tailed tits and siskins.

If the different types of food can be separated to some extent then more birds will be able to feed at the same time. This means a greater variety of birds in the garden, and more oppor-

FIGURE 21 *The magpie*

tunities for you to identify and study them.

Occasionally birds suffer from a type of food poisoning which they catch from one another. If you notice some individuals looking rather sick, scrub the bird table thoroughly and move it to another part of the garden so that no more birds become infected.

In spring and summer, birds can normally find plenty of food for themselves without being fed by man. When they are breeding they need to find natural food for their nestlings, which cannot digest as many types of food as their parents. It is therefore better not to put out food for birds for the six months from April to September (unless April is very cold). You would not be able to attract many birds to your garden in summer in any case, because they disperse into separate breeding territories. However, birds will always be glad of a supply

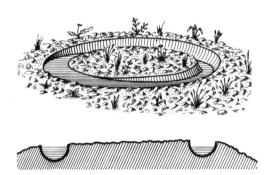

FIGURE 20 *A bird bath made from an old car tyre*

34

of water; this should be provided all the year round.

Bird baths

A bird bath can be made of concrete, but a variety of other materials will do just as well. A kitchen bowl makes a good bath. Scoop out a hole in the ground and put in the bowl so that its rim is level with the earth. Tread the surrounding soil well down to hold the bowl in position. A dust-bin lid is an alternative, or you can make a "pond" from an old car tyre cut in half lengthwise. Birds not only drink from these baths, they bathe too—and this can be great fun to watch.

If you feel that one day you might like to do some bird photography, now is the time to make provision for this by placing your food containers and bird bath in positions which will be suitable for photography. The most important consideration is that there should be sufficient light and that the sun should not shine directly into the lens.

There are many species of birds which can be fed, watched and photographed near the window but not all birds like to eat from a free-swinging container. As birds get used to your garden you will find they become less nervous of approaching the house and you may succeed in attracting them right on to your window-sill.

Food for birds

All sorts of scraps that you would normally throw away are attractive to birds. It is also possible to buy various suitable kinds of food. Nuts are very popular with tits, greenfinches and nuthatches. Greenfinches also like sunflower seeds but they

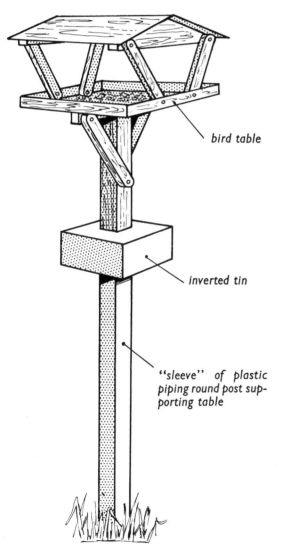

bird table

inverted tin

"sleeve" of plastic piping round post supporting table

FIGURE 22 *A bird table which is guaranteed to thwart squirrels, provided there are no overhanging branches*

35

A flock of blue tits enjoy an early morning bathe

leave the husks, which accumulate untidily on the ground. Grain attracts wood pigeons and collared doves. Small seeds of various kinds are eaten by hedge-sparrows and chaffinches. The fat off cuts of meat is ideal for a number of birds, and bones will bring into the garden magpies and perhaps even a kestrel. As for robins, they are especially partial to live mealworms. Many birds feed on berries in winter; a good way to supply these is to plant such bushes as cotoneaster and flowering currant.

There will come a day when all your preparations are completed and you can sit back and wait for the arrival of your guests. Patience is

necessary, because the birds of the neighbourhood have to "discover" the new feeding place for themselves. The time it takes them to find the new food supply depends on local conditions. If the street is lined with trees or there is a park near your home, you will not have to wait long, particularly if there is a spell of hard weather.

For most of the year the various species of birds keep more or less to themselves but during winter they often form flocks, which may contain several hundred birds. Both flocks of tits and flocks of finches travel about the countryside. Now and then one member of the flock strays and you may well succeed in attracting this

36

wanderer to your garden; if so, the rest of the flock will soon follow.

Sparrows and tits can be relied upon to be not only the first guests at your table but also your most constant visitors. The tits will provide a daily programme of acrobatics and, as well as enjoying their antics, you can start trying to identify the different species. Most handbooks list several species of tit, but those most commonly seen at a bird table are the great tit (dark head with white patch on each cheek), coal tit (white spot at nape of the neck) and blue tit (light blue cap or crown). Another likely visitor if there are trees near your garden is the nuthatch (black stripe through eye).

If you watch carefully you will soon discover that there are not only many different species at your food tables but that each bird has a personality of its own. There is the cheeky fellow who tries to crowd the others out, and there is the shy individualist who prefers to sit on a nearby branch watching others feed before daring to join the crowd.

Some people might argue that feeding birds during winter is not such a good idea after all. It is a biological fact that Nature has its own way of regulating the continuity of animal and plant life; during the

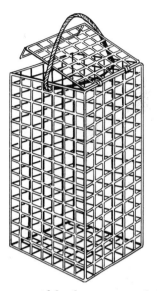

FIGURE 23 *Metal cage peanut-holder*

winter months the weaklings are eliminated. By feeding birds in the winter the weak ones are helped to survive and this may be to the detriment of the species as a whole.

FIGURE 24 *Spiral nut-holder*

37

This long-tailed tit has made her nest in a gorse bush but she might well be attracted into your garden

However, the balance of Nature is surely not going to be upset by feeding a small number of birds, and there can be no serious objection to it. As a means to becoming familiar with a number of species it is certainly a great help to the bird-watcher who is just beginning to learn about birds.

FIGURE 25 *The great tit*

38

CHAPTER FIVE

Practical Aids to Identifying Birds

Binoculars · Shape, size, patterning and colour · Naming the parts of a bird

HAVING A BIRD TABLE in your garden offers many chances for close observation. Identifying birds is largely a question of attention to detail and memorizing what you see. The best aid to memory is methodical note-taking, while rough sketches and brief descriptions written down *on the spot* are far more valuable than trying to carry things in your head. It is a good idea to have a notebook handy all the time, carry one in your pocket so that you are never without it. Watching birds while they remain in one place, such as at a bird table, gives you a chance to see a fair amount of detail with the naked eye. Sooner or later, however, you will need a pair of binoculars and this is the only aid to bird-watching which is expensive.

Binoculars

Some people refuse to use binoculars as they say that they make their eyes ache, give them headaches or even make them feel sick; this could be caused by faulty binoculars or by faulty eyesight, and in such a case it is best to seek advice from an optician.

When buying binoculars for bird-watching it is important to take their size and weight into account as well as their magnification. Sooner or later you will want to hold them steady in windy conditions so that weight is an important consideration. The power of binoculars is marked on the casing, for example as "8 × 30". The first figure indicates the power of enlargement and the second the size of the object lens, that is, the one you hold away from your eye. The larger this lens the bigger and heavier the binoculars are. Thus 7 × 50 and 12 × 50 glasses are rather large for carrying round your neck for long periods. The higher the magnification the more detail you will be able to see, but you must remember that the more a glass magnifies a bird the more it magnifies the movements of your hands too. It is difficult to hold steady a glass of 12 × magnification without a post or wall to prop it on. One other point to bear in mind is the amount of light that the binoculars pass to your eye. You can work this out quite simply by dividing the first figure into the second. For seeing birds well in normal light the second figure should be about four times as big as the first (e.g. 8 × 30), but if you want to look at birds in twilight the second figure should be

A goldfinch nest in a pear tree. This is the kind of sight which may reward patient watching in your garden

Binoculars allow you to watch wheatears like these. The male (left) is bringing food, while the female (right) is removing waste matter from the nest

relatively larger (e.g. 7 × 50). A popular size of field-glasses for general bird-watching is 8 × 30; these are light in weight and good models can be bought fairly inexpensively. When choosing your glasses try to select those which have "coated" lenses. These lenses are covered with a very fine blue film which increases the light power by 20 to 25 per cent, and as you may want to watch birds in poor light conditions, the extra expense is well worthwhile.

For quick adjustment, binoculars with central focusing are best as this enables both lenses to be focused simultaneously instead of adjusting each eye-piece separately. When you are trying to follow a bird in flight, this is obviously important.

All these suggestions refer to prismatic binoculars. A telescope can also be used but then a tripod is essential. Good telescopes are more expensive than binoculars and they are only of real value for carrying out observa-

The pied flycatcher which has distinctive black and white markings

tions from a fixed point. A bird-watcher must be mobile, and his aids to seeing must be reasonably light as well as of suitable magnification. Try to borrow various types of binoculars before you buy yourself a pair so that you can weigh the advantages of the various types against the disadvantages under the actual conditions in which you will be using them.

Shape, size, patterning and colour

Identifying birds is rather like working out a detective story. You

42

need to know what kinds of clue to follow and to concentrate on them in great detail. Size, shape, patterning and colour are all valuable clues. Take the question of size first of all: it may sound easy to guess the size of a bird, but light can play queer tricks. In fact, it is not easy to estimate the length of a bird in inches but it is easy to make estimates of *relative* size. Compare the bird you are watching with one that you are already familiar with. Is it about the same size as a sparrow, a blackbird or a pigeon, for example? Does it have an unusually long bill or tail?

The overall shape of a bird also helps you to keep a picture in your mind. Is it long and thin or short and dumpy? Has it long legs or short legs? Are its wings pointed or rounded at the tips? What is the shape of its tail? Having captured the shape of the

FIGURE 26 *Various shapes of tail (graduated, wedge-shaped, rounded, square-ended, notched, forked)*

bird in your mind, you will then start noticing pattern and colour. Perhaps your bird has a long tail—but has it any light bands across the end or higher up? Have the wings any kind of light colour as a bar? The back may appear uniform in colour until the bird flies off but when the wings are spread a light patch may be revealed just above the tail, on the rump.

As you become accustomed to noticing detail, you will start to observe that birds move in different

FIGURE 27 *Parts of a bird:*

1 *upper mandible*	15 *belly*
2 *lower mandible*	16 *tibia*
3 *chin*	17 *nostril*
4 *ear coverts*	18 *shoulder*
5 *lores*	19 *lesser wing coverts*
6 *forehead*	20 *median wing coverts*
7 *crown*	21 *greater wing coverts*
8 *nape*	22 *primary coverts*
9 *mantle*	23 *secondaries*
10 *back*	24 *tail*
11 *rump*	25 *primaries*
12 *upper tail coverts*	26 *ankle*
13 *throat*	27 *tarsus*
14 *breast*	28 *toes*

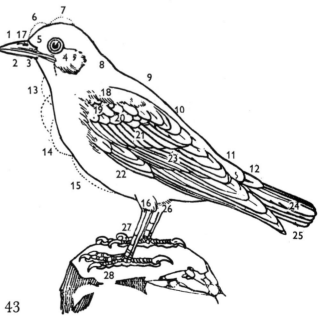

The oystercatcher which can be easily identified by its black and white markings

ways: some fly in a straight line with fast wing-beats, others glide and flap alternately to produce an undulating flight while others follow a zigzag course, and so on.

Naming the parts of a bird

It is difficult to take in and memorize all these details at once. Make notes as often as you can. You will find it much easier to do this once you have learned the correct terms for the different parts of a bird. You can then make a rough sketch and scribble down a brief description of each part of the bird. By using the correct terms you will save yourself time when you get home and want to compare your description with that of a reference book. It is useless making a note that a bird has a brown and white wing; when you come to look up the text-book, you will need to know precisely which part was white.

The shelduck which can be distinguished by its black-and-white pattern and chestnut breast

Figure 27 shows the various parts of a bird with the appropriate names. If you find them difficult to carry in your head when you first start, make a tracing of this sketch and carry it around with you. Using your own names for the parts of a bird instead of the correct ones is rather like making up your own words in a foreign language. They may mean something to you but they will mean nothing to others, and if you want to share your observations with other bird-watchers, you must learn to use the same language.

So far, we have only dealt with the garden as a place in which to learn the elements of bird-watching but not all species come to a garden and you will want to extend the range of your field-work. Expeditions for birds provide plenty of adventures and, once you can identify all the species which visit your garden, you should be well equipped for adding many more species to your list.

Chaffinch

Black redstart

Redstart

Blackbird

Songthrush

Spotted
flycatcher

Garden
warbler

Nightingale

Blackcap

Robin

Pied wagtail

Chiffchaff

Swallow

House martin

Starling

Swift

Kestrel

Cuckoo

Sparrowhawk

Magpie

Collared dove

Wood pigeon

FIGURE 28 *These birds may all be seen in parts of Britain during the spring*

CHAPTER SIX

Expeditions for Birds

How much does a bird see? ·
Various habitats · *Making notes*

IN THE SEARCH for birds it is best to go in easy stages. Once you have explored the garden thoroughly, you can go to the nearest park. It is not much use looking for birds in the patches of turf one finds here and there between towering blocks of flats and offices. A single tree on a lawn will not attract many birds, but parks usually have shrubberies and plenty of cover or, possibly, an ornamental lake or pond. Some artificial lakes in parks are a great attraction to wildfowl, and one of the easiest ways of learning about various species of duck is to visit a town park. You can get quite close to the ducks, and there are often many more species side by side on a town lake than you would find on a stretch of water in the country.

It is a mistake to think that you will never see a "new" bird in the heart of a city. What could be more exciting than to see a black redstart or kestrel in London? Apart from species which like cliff-like buildings, there is always a chance that birds which prefer more open country may fly across the city on their way to another stretch of country. You never know what you will see if you remain alert all the time.

There are a number of species which have moved into the towns, adapting themselves to the noise and bustle of modern civilization. Until the middle of the last century black-birds were not seen in towns, and it is hard to say why they moved out of the woods into the built-up areas. Wood-pigeons, or ring doves as they are sometimes called, have also moved into our city squares; in such surroundings they are at least comparatively free from a sudden attack by a hawk. Magpies and jays have also taken to living in towns and are becoming quite cheeky in this respect. More and more great spotted woodpeckers are coming to bird tables in gardens; what other species will move into built-up areas?

Each one of the species found in towns can, of course, also be found in wilder and more natural surroundings

The tufted duck which is often seen on lakes in town parks

but their behaviour is bound to be different. The town wood-pigeon pays no attention when car doors are slammed but the country wood-pigeon is a shy bird and even the snapping of a twig sends it off at great speed. The town mallard is so accustomed to people at close quarters that it scarcely bothers to waddle out of the way when strollers approach it on a path in the park; but a mallard resting on the bank of a quiet stretch of the river will be up and

FIGURE 29 *You may see a black redstart like this in London*

49

away almost before you have had a chance of seeing its dark green head.

The country bird-watcher has to take a great deal of care or he will be detected long before he has had a chance to get a look at the bird he is anxious to identify. Creeping stealthily through the undergrowth sounds a good idea but it usually results in upsetting a great many animals who are listening for every sound. It is a fact that a group of people, however noisy, do not frighten woodland creatures nearly as much as a single individual who is trying to be very quiet. Animals hear loud noises from a distance and retreat into their own homes in good time. To be suddenly confronted by an unexpected intruder at close quarters is much more alarming and they react accordingly, often fleeing in terror and exposing themselves to greater danger from predators. An individual bird-watcher causes less disturbance generally if he goes to the area where he hopes to

find something and then sits down, preferably near cover so that he merges into the background, and waits patiently without moving. After a while the birds return and behave quite naturally. Sudden or jerky movements can ruin all your plans.

How much does a bird see?

Naturally you want to get as close as possible to your subject but this is not always easy. It is no use approaching a bird in a straight line; all birds dislike this even if they are used to living in a town. A bird's eye is extremely sensitive to movement. It is possible for a bird to register about one hundred and fifty different impressions in one second; a comparable figure for the human eye lies between twenty and seventy.

Ciné photography takes this fact into account. Normal film is projected at a speed of about twenty-four frames per second, giving the human eye an impression of normal speed. A film of scurrying mice shown to an owl at this speed would leave no impression of speed; the mice would appear to the owl to be a group of more or less still objects.

There is another advantage which birds have over humans: the angle of their field of vision is much larger than ours. Figure 31 shows the

FIGURE 30 *A skylark takes off in alarm*

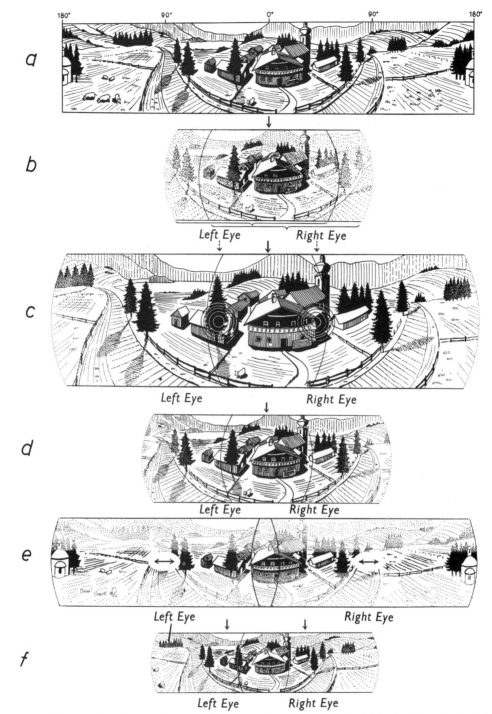

FIGURE 31 *Comparative fields of vision: the curved lines indicate the field of vision of the left and right eyes respectively. Notice how the vision of both eyes "overlaps" the centre. This overlap is largest in the human eye, smallest in the eyes of a wader, but the wader's vision covers almost the full circle. a: panoramic view of 360 degrees; b: as seen through the human eye; c: as seen through the eyes of a bird of prey; d: as seen through the eyes of an owl; e: as seen through the eyes of a wader; f: as seen through the eyes of a song bird*

The turtle dove, a summer visitor recognised by its patterned neck and distinctive song

difference between the scope of the human eye and that of various birds. Yet another point is worth remembering as you approach a bird: try to have the light behind you. This helps to deceive the bird about your size and in bright sunlight it throws the light on to the bird instead of directly into your eyes. A bird seen as a black silhouette can be very difficult to identify. Ideally, you should try to position yourself so that at the end of your approach the bird is directly in front of you; it is then bound to come some way towards you as it flies off. This gives you a chance to memorize the colour of its breast, the patternings on the wings,

52

the shape of its tail and so on. In fact, it is time to get out your notebook and make the necessary entries.

Various habitats

After a time you will get to know which birds you can expect to see on different kinds of expeditions and according to the time of year. For instance, in midwinter you may find large flocks of lapwing on estuaries, but by mid-March you may find individual pairs already taking up territory in ploughed fields. When you have become familiar with birds of one place or *habitat* you will want to try another habitat so that you can add more species to your list.

The best thing to do is to refer to a local ordnance map and work to a plan. Clearings in the middle of woods or small ponds are always worth investigating; damp meadows and marshy land may well harbour birds you do not normally see in woodlands; heaths, moors, downs, mudflats, lakes and man-made reservoirs all provide a habitat for various species. Some of these places are well off the beaten track but good maps are easily obtained and every bird-watcher should be able to read a map.

Making notes

As you extend your boundaries of

FIGURE 32 *Pond birds. From left: female teal, coot, dabchick, drake mallard*

53

The curlew which breeds on moorland but feeds in winter on mudflats

bird-watching you will come across more species which are unfamiliar. When you go for a day's tramp you will want to travel light and not be burdened with heavy reference books for identifying what you see. This

54

The redshank, another bird which visits estuaries in winter

means that at the end of the day you will be entirely dependent on the notes which you have made on the spot, while in the field. You will see so much that is new; you will forget details as the day goes on and new sights crowd in upon you; unless you discipline yourself to use your note-book, you will be a very disappointed bird-watcher when it comes to using the textbooks. There is nothing more maddening than to find that you may have seen a rare species but you cannot be certain because your notes make no mention of the one feature which is diagnostic. Did you forget to write it down? Did you actually see it? Your memory fails you and because the detail is not in your notes you will never be certain.

There is one golden rule about identifying birds: make notes on the spot referring to every part of the bird you can see and to every mannerism, gait or stance that you notice. Scraps of paper get lost on a day's outing and a field notebook is much safer; it also provides a semi-

Red-backed shrikes, rare summer visitors to southern England

permanent record. An ordinary exercise book will do, but choose a size that will fit your pocket. For each excursion you should head the page with the date, locality, weather conditions (wind, cloud, temperature) and the time of the beginning and ending of the expedition. Extensive notes of your observations can then be listed. Small sketches, however rough, are always useful. If you are doubtful about the accuracy of your observation, put a large question mark in the margin. You can then check your notes with a reference book when you get home. If you are puzzled by anything you see it is always worth referring to the textbooks; they may give you a clue as to what you have seen and, with this in mind, you will be able to follow it up next time you have an opportunity in the field.

The common sandpiper, well known for its bobbing mannerism

The bittern. You may have to go to Norfolk to find one

A field notebook soon becomes dirty, crumpled and torn, even if it is between hard covers. It should be treated as only a semi-permanent record. You never know when you will want to refer back to field notes; it may be months or even years later, and so it is well worth transferring your field notes into some more permanent form of record. You may prefer a file with loose sheets of paper or a set of cards or even a permanent record book. It depends on how you want to arrange your notes for easy reference. You may decide to keep sections for bird song, courtship, nesting behaviour and so on. It is entirely a matter of personal preference depending on your own particular interest. Remember that notes are made to be used and so, whatever system you adopt, it should enable you to find the particular note you are looking for without too much trouble or delay. Carefully assembled notes are a treasured storehouse of information and of memorable occasions, and one day they may even be of use to a professional ornithologist —so make them orderly and legible.

FIGURE 33 *An example of small sketches made for subsequent reference*

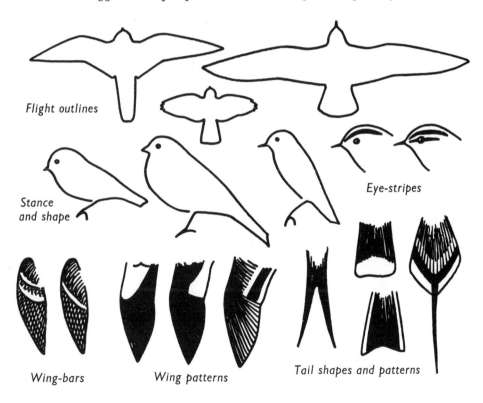

Flight outlines

Stance and shape

Eye-stripes

Wing-bars   Wing patterns   Tail shapes and patterns

CHAPTER SEVEN

Nestboxes

How to make nestboxes
Where to place them

WE OFTEN HEAR about the housing shortage for humans, but has it occurred to you that we are continually creating a housing shortage for birds? Natural habitats disappear as more and more land is taken for industrial development. Ponds and marshes are drained, trees and hedges are uprooted and Nature is rarely left undisturbed. It is increasingly difficult for birds to find sheltered sites for nesting, and even where parks and gardens are available, they are usually kept much too tidy for the natural requirements of birds.

There is something that you can do to help overcome this shortage and at the same time you will be doing yourself a good turn. By putting up nestboxes in your garden you can provide a safe place for birds to rear their young and, incidentally, provide yourself with a first-class view of behaviour at the nest. Several species are only too ready to use nestboxes provided they are made of suitable material and to certain specifications. Each species has its own requirements and the hole-nesters are very particular about the size of the entrance hole. When making a nestbox you should try to imitate Nature as closely as possible, and you can even choose which species you want to encourage by making the box according to its requirements.

The British Trust for Ornithology have issued an excellent pamphlet on nestboxes which includes information about the sizes of entrance hole appropriate to various species. For instance: the great spotted woodpecker and starling use a 2 in. (50 mm.) hole, house sparrow $1\frac{1}{4}$ in. (37 mm.), nuthatch $1\frac{1}{8}$-$1\frac{1}{2}$ in. (28-37 mm.), tree sparrow $1\frac{1}{8}$ in. (28 mm.), tits $1\frac{1}{8}$ in. (28 mm.) and so on.

These dimensions were discovered by quite a simple experiment. Tame birds of various species were allowed to get at their food only after passing through various-sized holes. In this way it was possible to find out which hole was acceptable to each species and which was rejected.

Home-made nestboxes are by no

A pair of swallows which built their nest in a coil of wire hanging in a farmyard shed. The male (left)
is identified by his longer tail feathers

means a modern invention. In the valley of the River Emms in Germany there are mediæval castles which have nest holes built into the stonework; young birds used to be considered a great delicacy, and in times of siege they were a welcome addition to the larder. Dutch paintings of the six-teenth and seventeenth centuries frequently show nestboxes on the eaves of houses and on steeples; most of these appear to have been made of clay. There are also many paintings by old masters showing wheels and iron frameworks being used as founda-tions for storks' nests.

How to make nestboxes

Nestboxes should be made out of well-seasoned timber as this does not warp. The timber should be $\frac{3}{4}$-1 in. (20-25 mm.) thick. It is best not to plane the inside of the box but to leave it rough to enable the birds to get a foothold. The roof should over-hang by $\frac{1}{2}$ in. (12 mm.) at the back and sides, and by 1 in. (25 mm.) at the front. If it can be covered by roofing felt, so much the better, but try to use one which does not contain too much tar.

To provide drainage, you should either bore two small holes, about $\frac{1}{4}$-in. (6 mm.) diameter, in the floor or make a slit; this is done by setting the floor back for about $\frac{1}{8}$ in. (3 mm.) from the front—but if you do this, make sure that the floor is on a slight slope.

There are various types of nestbox,

FIGURE 34 *A simple nestbox can be made from timber cut to the above pattern. Pieces A, B, C help to strengthen the front wall. D holds it in place inside the box*

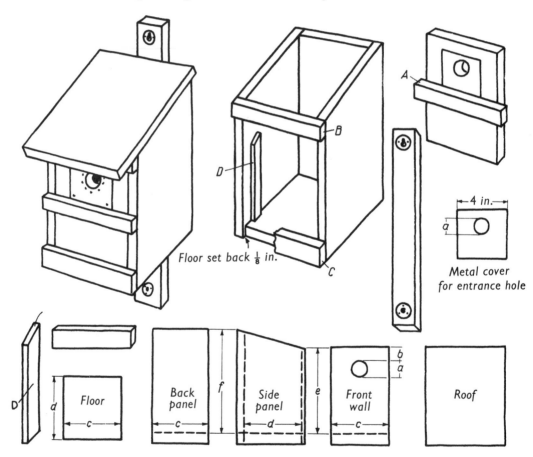

Floor set back $\frac{1}{8}$ in.

Metal cover for entrance hole

Floor

Back panel

Side panel

Front wall

Roof

many of which are mentioned in the B.T.O. pamphlet, but Figure 34 shows you a type which has been found suitable for various species. The dimensions vary according to the species you wish to encourage but the principles of construction are the same. The following table lists the requirements of some species:

Species	Entrance Hole	Depth	Floor Dimensions
(Measurements in inches)			
Nuthatch, tits	$1\frac{1}{8}$–$1\frac{1}{2}$	5	4×4
Redstart	$1\frac{1}{2}$–2	5	4×4
Great spotted woodpecker	2	12	5×5
Little owl	4	12	$7\frac{1}{2} \times 7\frac{1}{2}$

Try to build the front panel of the box in such a way that it can be removed; this enables you to clean the box out after each season. A box which cannot be cleaned out at least once a year is useless as the old nesting material is a breeding place for all kinds of parasites. Remember that timber swells in wet weather and the front panel should be rather on the small side to allow for this. It is also a good idea to protect the entrance hole with a thin piece of aluminium or galvanized iron; starlings or woodpeckers can be a nuisance if they try to enlarge the hole when you already have a pair of tits in residence.

Where to place nestboxes

Birds, as well as humans, have their preferences when it comes to choosing a site for their home. They do not like damp or draughty corners and they mostly prefer semi-shade, although some prefer a more open position than others. The entrance hole should not face into the prevailing wind nor into direct sun during the hottest part of the day. Make sure that the box is securely fixed so that wind and rain do not dislodge it, and try to fix it at a slightly forward angle so that rainwater runs off the roof and does not get trapped at the back. The easiest method of fixing is to fasten a batten of wood to the back of the box so that it projects above and below the box; nails or screws can then be driven through the top and bottom of the batten into a tree or post. Wooden pegs or long aluminium nails should be used if the tree is still growing and is of value as timber.

For birds which prefer a more open type of box, the front panel can be made so that it covers only half the front (Figure 35). This open type is

This wren, settling down at dusk to brood her young, has built her nest in a bundle of fishing nets hanging in a shed

best fitted directly against a wall or building and, once again, exposure to prevailing wind or too much sun should be avoided.

It is a good idea to hide the box, for example among creepers growing on the wall, so that birds' enemies do not see it. The birds that nest in this kind of box include robin, spotted flycatcher, redstart and pied wagtail.

Swallows, house martins and swifts have been successfully attracted to ledges and open nestboxes. These simple boxes, shown in Figure 36, are very easy to make. As these birds like living with plenty of neighbours, it is a good idea to put up several boxes near to each other. If the

64

weather should be dry in May and June, make sure that water is available, or keep a patch of soil very damp, as the birds need this moisture for making their nests, which are constructed of mud.

These shallow, open nestboxes will also attract blackbirds, song thrushes and spotted flycatchers. Even a simple ledge will be adopted by one of these birds. Sometimes birds find a platform for a nest inside a garden shed or garage, and start building while the door or window is open. If possible you should then leave the window open so that the birds can carry on nesting and rear their young.

Yet another group of birds may be

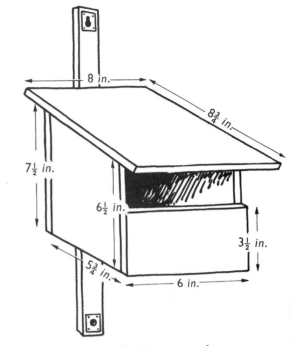

FIGURE 35 *Some birds prefer the open nestbox*

FIGURE 36 *Swallows do not need elaborate nestboxes. These simple boxes are very easy to make*

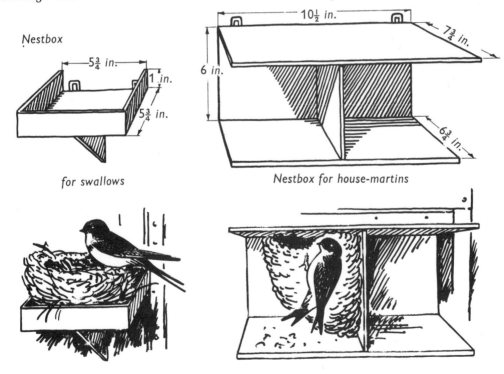

Nestbox

for swallows

Nestbox for house-martins

FIGURE 37 *Two types of nesting "pocket"; they must be securely tied*

attracted to your garden if you give them a little encouragement: these are the hedge and shrub nesters. If, instead of having fences to mark the boundary of your home, you plant hedges or leave some shrubs which are kept not too well pruned, you will have some natural nesting sites which can be supplemented by artificial nesting "pockets". Make a small bunch of twigs and tie them to a post or tree; broom, gorse or any kind of evergreen is suitable (see Figure 37). If you leave the twigs a little loose, rather than bound tightly, birds can get in and out of these pockets and may decide to build nests in them.

The simplest of all "nestboxes" to make are household containers such as old kettles and watering-cans. These are taken over by the same species that use open-fronted nest-boxes, and in particular by robins, which are famous for rearing families in pots and pans. These objects should be put up in thick bushes where they are well hidden from predators. They should be well above the ground, and be firmly secured to the surrounding branches. They must slope in such a way that any rainwater that enters the opening runs out again.

Birds take time to get accustomed to their surroundings and they tend to be suspicious of any change: for this reason it is advisable to have your nestboxes in position throughout the winter. Birds may even roost in them and if they get used to perching on them and perhaps entering them, they may well choose them as nesting sites in the breeding season. Should your boxes be ignored for several months, it is best not to move them unless you are certain that you have made a mistake and sited them incorrectly; it is much

Young blackcaps waiting to be fed

more likely that the birds are still suspicious of them, and if you move the boxes this will only make them more suspicious.

The first time you see a pair of birds going in and out of one of your boxes, carrying nesting material, you will feel very excited and doubtless you will later be tempted to open the box to see how many eggs have been laid. It is much safer to leave the box alone, but if you cannot restrain your curiosity, make sure that neither of the adults is near the

Feeding time. Young swallows are always hungry

box when you open it. It would be very disappointing to have your first pair desert their nest.

One word of warning about nest-boxes. By attracting birds to nest in your garden, you make yourself responsible for their safety. Make sure that no predators can reach the boxes.

It is tempting to fit a perch to the front of the box, but don't forget that this is equally tempting for predators. A squirrel or a cat will find it easier to reach into the box from a perch. The approach to a nestbox can be protected by tying thorny twigs or gorse just below the box or by cutting sharp bits of tin into the shape of a ring (Figure 38). To prevent the box being opened, fix small hooks to each side of the box, to fit into eyes on the lid when it is closed.

A garden with plenty of birds is something of which most ornithologists dream. Expeditions are always exciting, but if you really want to study birds it is a great help to have them near at hand. Bird song, nest building, incubation, feeding of young and fledging—all these are available if you succeed in attracting birds to your garden.

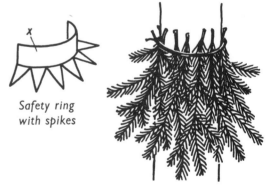

Safety ring with spikes

FIGURE 38 *Devices to keep cats away*

CHAPTER EIGHT

Hobbies Connected with Birds

Bird photography · Subjects for the beginner · Using a flashlight · Trial and error · Watching from a hide

BIRDS APPEAL TO people for a large variety of reasons. After you have made some headway with identifying birds, you may decide to turn your attention to one of the hobbies connected with bird-watching, such as bird photography or recording the sounds birds make. No one can decide for you how to develop your interest in birds, but sometimes it is useful to have suggestions. Your own interests and enthusiasm will lead you in the direction you want to go, but this chapter may give you ideas about what to try next.

Bird photography

This may appear at first sight to be a job for experts only, but amateurs may achieve quite a lot providing they have common sense and are prepared to devote time to making careful preparations. Have you ever thought of illustrating your field notes with photographs instead of sketches? It is more costly but you can have a lot of fun in the process, and if you are any good at photography the results will be far better than amateur drawings.

What kind of equipment will you need and how much will it cost? Fortunately the most expensive apparatus is not necessarily the most suitable for this type of photography. All kinds of special equipment can be bought, but for the person who regards bird photography as a hobby, an ordinary camera will be adequate. Try to buy one which is suitable for the addition of a telescopic lens and flash outfit. These are not essential for the beginner but they are useful additions once you know how to take satisfactory pictures. An exposure meter is, however, essential; it is true that many good photographs have been taken without the help of an exposure meter, but light can be deceptive and, when your luck turns, the hoped for prize-winning picture will be ruined by a wrong exposure.

Birds are fickle creatures; it is not

easy to predict what they will do. It is up to you to make sure that those things which *are* under your control, such as exposure and focus, are accurate. A tripod is one method of overcoming the possibility of a last-minute gust of wind which may ruin your picture through camera shake. A glittering tripod may startle a bird, so make sure that your tripod has a matt finish and if necessary paint the chromium parts. It may not look as attractive but it will be much more useful; after all, you are photographing birds rather than carrying around a portable bird-scarer.

Some bird photographers use cameras that take $2\frac{1}{4} \times 2\frac{1}{4}$ in. (6×6 cm.) pictures. However, these tend to be more expensive than smaller cameras, and less suitable for photographing moving birds. Many excellent shots have been obtained using 35 mm. cameras. Generally speaking, the more you enlarge a picture the higher is the risk of "grain" showing on the print. Photographic materials are continually being improved and, in many cases, it is the man developing the film who can get the best out of the picture. You cannot do better than go to a reputable firm and ask their advice about equipment and materials. Commercial firms are naturally anxious to encourage amateur photographers, and if you tell them the sort of pictures you wish to take, they will do everything they can to see that you are successful.

Subjects for the beginner

Like everything else, photography needs learning stage by stage. Before attempting flight shots or birds at the nest, try to get some good photographs of birds at your bird table. Most birds come to the table at more or less the same time each day and you can practise getting them in the viewfinder, calculate the distance for focus, read your light meter and so on, before actually taking a picture. Do take particular care that the bird is going to be sharply in focus. The average camera allows for close-ups to be taken from a distance of about

FIGURE 39 *In real life birds will not, unfortunately, pose for the photographer*

70

An expert photographer can produce a photograph as good as this one which shows a linnet with her young

three feet (1 m.) If the bird table is positioned just outside a window, it may not be too difficult to take pictures from inside the house through the open window.

Birds are as suspicious of unaccustomed noise as they are of sudden movement, and it may not be practical to release the camera shutter by hand without the birds being aware of

71

your presence. In this case, some kind of remote control can be arranged. The necessary apparatus can be bought, but with a little ingenuity a much cheaper version can be made at home. Figure 40 shows how this is done. Remember to make quite sure that the thread can neither break nor become tangled at the crucial moment. A fine fishing-line is strong and suitable for the purpose.

A disadvantage of using remote-control shutter release is that the mechanism has to be reset after every picture. This may well mean disturbing the birds from their food but, providing you disappear again quickly, they should return without undue delay.

Using a flashlight

Flashlight equipment makes you independent of light conditions and this, of course, is a great advantage. The flash attachment can be fixed to your camera, but if you position the light at a slight angle to the object

FIGURE 40 *A home-made device which enables you to bring your camera within about three feet* (1 *m.*) *of your bird-table. The thread is drawn through a staple to prevent it from getting tangled.*

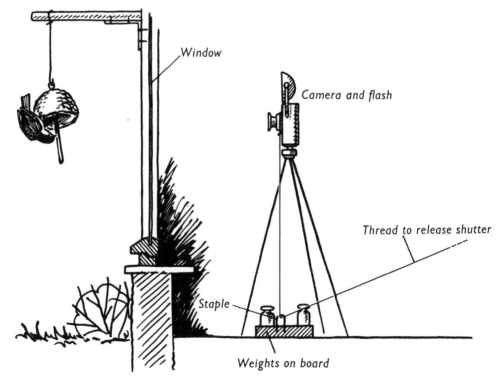

Window

Camera and flash

Thread to release shutter

Staple

Weights on board

The red-throated diver—sometimes the surrounding cover makes a good setting for the photograph

your pictures will have much more depth. When using the flash for close-ups it is best to have a film of fairly low sensitivity in the camera. You might think that a flash would be bound to frighten a bird away but, in fact, this does not usually happen because the flash appears as not much more than a flash of lightning and is over so rapidly that most birds do not react to it.

When you have taken a number of satisfactory pictures you will probably want to get the birds bigger in the picture, to get really large close-ups. Even this is possible but, once again, careful preparations are necessary. It is obviously necessary to move the tripod close to the bird table. It must be level with the birds and the lens should be pointed at the most likely spot. As far as the birds are concerned, the lens will "shine" and the whole apparatus will probably be regarded with the utmost suspicion. Anything which you can do to reduce this

73

suspicion will help your final results. Obviously it is not a good idea to leave your equipment in the garden, waiting for the birds to become used to it near the table, so a little deception is called for. A dummy tripod and camera can be made out of old wood with a pocket mirror to represent the lens. The dummy equipment should be moved nearer and nearer to the table, reducing the distance by easy stages until the birds pay no further attention to it, even when it is close to the table. You are then ready to put your skill to the test and, having checked your exposure (aperture and shutter speed) and focus, your patience should be rewarded.

When the breeding season starts you might want to try photographing nests. Unfortunately most birds nest in situations away from direct light and flashlight is usually necessary. They also tend to be tucked under cover at heights which make photography difficult and there is much to

A pheasant at her nest

A portrait of a whinchat perched on a gorse bush

FIGURE 41 *A model barn owl which may be used to get action pictures*

be said for encouraging birds to nest in positions suitable for photography. This can be done by putting up nest-boxes in places where you can photograph them from a hide. Remember that birds are suspicious of any strange object, particularly near the nest. It might take them a few days to get used to a hide; you should take it down if the birds show any signs of agitation.

If a pair of breeding birds are disturbed for more than a very short time they may well desert the nest for good. Not only will you have lost your photographs but the birds will have to start looking for a new nesting place all over again, and because they are now behind schedule they may have missed the time when food for their young is most plentiful. All in all, their chances of successfully rearing a family could have been badly upset.

Trial and error

Photography, like bird-watching, is something which cannot be learned from books alone. You have to try it and learn from your mistakes. As you gain experience you develop techniques and "tricks" which are all your own. You will need all the "tricks" for photographing birds in the field because, under completely wild conditions, birds are less likely to be accustomed to the presence of human beings. Nests tend to be built in situations where there is at least some protection from predators and weather; one might almost add that they are built in sites protected from the photographer.

It is tempting to do a little "gardening" and trim some of the leaves and branches which hide the nest from your lens. But, if you do this, the bird may desert, and even if it ignores your interference, it will have lost its natural protection. Jays, magpies, squirrels and cats will all be able to see the nest more easily. Very young fledglings may die from heat-stroke if they are exposed to much direct sunlight; a few branches of leaves shading the nest make all the difference.

A bird chooses its nest site for

nearly all the reasons which make it difficult for you to photograph it. Any outside interference is, therefore, bound to be detrimental in one way or another. The real bird-lover refrains from disturbing birds in any way. It is better to forgo the chance of getting a photograph than to risk losing a young family of birds. You should not attempt to photograph the nests of rare birds until you have a great deal of experience, and even then you must by law get permission from the Natural Environment Research Council.

Birds coming in to land make excellent action shots. Since they land facing into the wind, position yourself accordingly. Birds react to wind rather like a weather-vane and they face into it, even when perching, in order to avoid getting their feathers ruffled. Anticipation of what the bird will do, exactly where it will be in focus with the light at a slight angle and how long it is likely to remain thus, all these points are worth studying before you try your luck with an action shot.

There is one method of inducing action amongst birds which has been used by photographers with some success. You may have noticed that birds tend to become excited when an owl appears on the scene; try placing a model owl in a rather conspicuous place, close to some branches, and you may find that the bird population

FIGURE 42 *A home-made tent*

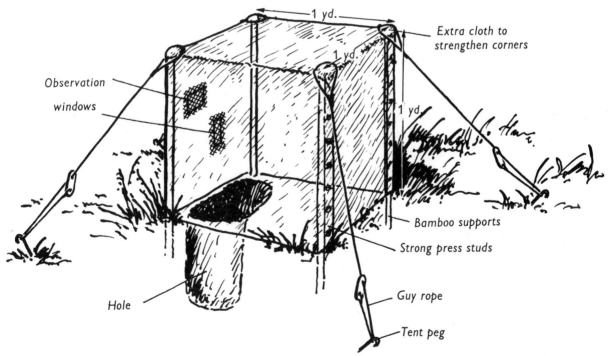

1 yd.

Extra cloth to strengthen corners

Observation windows

1 yd.

1 yd.

Bamboo supports

Strong press studs

Hole

Guy rope

Tent peg

of the neighbourhood arrives to "mob" the owl. Often the birds are so busy scolding at the owl that they pay no attention to the photographer. This is not a trick which should be tried too often in the same neighbourhood or for too long at a time because it causes considerable disturbance to the birds, and if they get too upset they may leave altogether.

If you are lucky enough to possess a telescopic lens you can have a lot of fun stalking your subjects. This is tremendously exciting, but you will need a large measure of luck as well as skill. Wild animals and birds have only one means of self-preservation when they are thoroughly alarmed and this is to flee. Each one has a certain distance at which it likes to keep from potential danger. Imagine a circle round a bird or animal. The size of the circle varies with different species and is also determined by various biological factors; a bird will take flight if anything breaks into this circle and a large animal will try to flee—but its instinct for flight may turn into aggression if it is cornered.

Watching from a hide

To see everything without being seen should be your aim whether you are taking photographs or just watching birds. A hide can help you to get really close to birds as it is virtually a method of disguising yourself in the field. Sometimes it is possible to construct a hide out of branches and twigs, bracken or some natural foliage, near the spot where you expect to see the particular bird you are stalking. A light, portable hide is obviously an advantage if you are going on long expeditions and a small two-man tent is suitable. Figure 42 shows a serviceable tent which can easily be made at home.

The tent should be of a dull brown, green or grey colour so that it does not stand out against a natural background. The following materials are necessary: 15 ft. (5 m.) of waterproof and lightproof cloth 3 ft. (1 m.) wide, 4 stout bamboo canes 4 ft. (120 cm.) long, 4 guy ropes and 4 tent pegs. The back of the tent is fastened with stout press-studs to prevent the material from flapping and frightening the birds. A little soil heaped along the bottom edges of the tent will stabilise it in a wind, and by stitching extra material over each of the four corners, added strength is given where the stress may be greatest. None of these things weigh much and they can be carried quite easily on long expeditions. It is well worth adding a small trowel to your equipment for digging up soil to heap along the bottom of the tent, and also to make depressions for your feet inside the tent so that you can sit more comfortably.

It is a good idea to have observation windows on two sides of the tent so that you can see a bird as it approaches. The height of these observation windows should be dictated by your own comfort; try sitting inside the hide and mark the material at a convenient height before you cut it. The slits should then be covered with gauze; you will be able to see through the gauze but the birds will not see you, and you can arrange the gauze so that the camera lens will protrude through it. It is worth making small cloth "blinds" to unroll over the gauze, from the inside of the hide, in bad weather; this adds to your comfort in windy or wet weather.

Equipped with such a portable tent it is possible to observe and photograph even the most elusive birds. Once you know the regular haunts and habits of the species you want to observe from the hide, all you need do is to sit inside and wait patiently. Providing you have done your field-work well and erected your hide carefully, your patience should be rewarded.

FIGURE 43 *Observation windows like this one enable you to watch the birds without being detected*

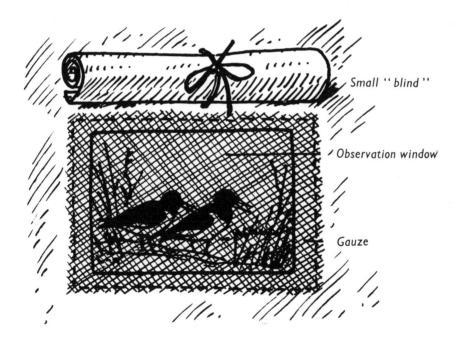

Small "blind"

Observation window

Gauze

CHAPTER NINE

Studies in the Breeding Season

Nest-building · Nests and eggs ·
Egg-laying, incubation and fledging

YOUR FIRST SPRING as a bird-watcher presents a bewildering choice of activities, there is so much to look at and so much to learn. Everything seems to happen all at once. There is an influx of migrants with calls, songs and plumage all to be identified; there are courtship displays, nest-building, egg-laying and soon there is the excitement of watching adult birds feeding their young families. Your field notebook becomes a mass of entries on all kinds of subjects. Try to keep records of all that you observe and, with any luck, by the end of the season, you will have answers to some of the following questions:

1. What is the cock's reaction to other birds of his species?
2. Is he able to distinguish at once between males and females?
3. Have the hens any particular mannerisms that make them easily recognizable?
4. At what distance does the cock recognize the hen?
5. Does he try to impress her by certain behaviour or display?
6. Do males and females have any special calls during courtship?
7. How many variations of song has the cock?
8. Has the cock a special form of song which he uses in one particular place only?
9. Do singing habits change according to (*a*) the time of day; (*b*) weather conditions; (*c*) during the time of nest-building and egg-laying; (*d*) during incubation?

All these points have interested ornithologists for many years. Charles Darwin thought that since the cock bird is the more colourful of the species, the hen chooses the one which shows the brightest plumage and has the loudest voice. This has since been disproved but exactly what influences her choice is still not quite clear.

Very early in the year the female robin goes in search of a mate and she may visit many territories before she finds a male that is to her liking. She approaches him directly and does not withdraw even if he shows aggression and tries to chase her away. Cock and hen both display their red breast-feathers and they puff and sway before each other for long periods. At last the cock gives in and follows her, twittering quietly. From now until the mating season they live amicably in the same territory and although they recognize each other at a distance of thirty yards, they do not take much notice of each other at this stage. It is thought that a male robin never refuses a female although he may appear to do so at first.

Nest-building

In a number of species pairing off and nest-building take place almost simultaneously. In some species a large part of the nest is built by the male before the final choice of partner is made; this is the case with herons and wrens. In others, the nest-building is carried out entirely

A golden oriole at its nest. These nests, usually slung under forked branches, can be seen in Europe

by the female. By keeping regular watch on birds near your home you can build up a set of records which will add to your knowledge about even the most familiar species.

1. Who chooses the nest site?
2. How far away is the nest from the song post on which the male perches regularly?
3. Do both cock and hen build the nest?
4. Where does the building material come from?
5. What type of material is used?
6. How many flights are made before the nest is completed and how long does it take to build a nest?
7. During which part of the day are the birds most actively engaged in nest-building?
8. Do all birds of the same species build nests at the same time?
9. Is the completion of the nest influenced by weather conditions?

The female hen harrier carrying nest material. She continued adding to the nest until the young were half-grown

10. Are there any delays due to prolonged disputes over territory?

All these questions cover some of the most important points in bird behaviour, and you will have your work cut out to find the answers to them. Take the question of nesting material: first you watch one of the birds arriving at the nest site carrying some material, and this is often the first indication that a nest is in the process of being built. You wait to see if more material is brought in and then you try to follow the bird back to the site from which it is gathering material. All this takes time because all nests are not made of one material: some are lined with mud or animal hair, some are decorated with bits of moss or lichen and birds have been known to pull threads from a woollen garment left to dry on the clothes-line. Tracking down the materials used by birds is rather like a detective story and it all takes time. For this reason it is best to concentrate on those species near your home so that you do not waste time going long distances before reaching the nest sites.

Birds know by instinct when and how to build their nests. The urge to build is as much inborn as the urge to mate and rear a young brood. Materials and sites are influenced by the character of the country in which the bird builds, and the same species

FIGURE 44 *The hedge-sparrow, a bird which lays 4-5 eggs*

may have different nesting habits in different surroundings. Some birds appear to decorate their nests for no particular reason and one wonders why they should do this. Just why should a ringed plover, for instance, put pebbles and little bits of shell around its nest?

Nests and eggs

The list below contains some information about nests and eggs of birds which you are most likely to find nesting near your home. It is a good idea to check your observations with this information.

Song-thrush Nest is cup-shaped and lined with wood and saliva. 4–5 eggs.
Blackbird Nest is cup-shaped and lined with an inner layer of dry grass. 4–5 eggs, often only 3.
House-sparrow and Starling Usually nest is in holes or cavities. Nest lined with straw or feathers. 4–6 eggs.
Hedge-sparrow Nest is rather a loose

FIGURE 45 *The tawny owl*

structure of twigs, grass, roots, etc. 4–5 eggs.

Great Tit and Blue Tit Nesting holes often contain moss and the nest is usually lined with hair, wool or down. 5 or 6–11 or more eggs.

Long-tailed Tit Nests in thick thorn or holly, also in trees overgrown with ivy or clematis. Nest shaped like a large egg with a small entrance near the top. 6–12 eggs.

Robin Nest is often a hole or cavity, cleverly concealed and always lined with soft material. 4–6 eggs.

Wren Nest is almost spherical with only a tiny entrance hole, made of moss and leaves, lined with feathers. 5–6 eggs.

Great Spotted Woodpecker Bores a nesting hole in a tree, no nesting material. 4–7 eggs.

Little Owl and Tawny Owl Nest is often in holes and cavities with no nesting material. 2–4 eggs.

Magpie Nest is almost completely round, usually in tall trees, often with a dome of sticks; it could be mistaken for a squirrel's drey. 5–8 eggs.

Some species repeatedly build their nests in dangerous positions. Great crested grebes, for instance, usually build not far from the edge of a lake or large pool; the nest is built on a floating mass of decayed water weed, and when the waters flood the birds try building the nest up with more twigs and sticks but they often lose the battle and have to start building all over again. Avocets also build close to water and the rising tide frequently engulfs their nests. These examples may disprove the theory that birds know instinctively which sites to choose but it proves that bird behaviour is complex and that we still have a great deal to learn.

Egg-laying, incubation and fledging

After nest-building comes the laying of eggs, the incubation period and the hatching and fledging of the young family. Once again a series of questions may help you to concentrate your observations in an effort to find the answers:

1. How much time elapses between the completion of the

84

nest and the laying of the first egg?

2. Do unfavourable weather conditions delay egg-laying?

3. Do hens of the same species lay their eggs at the same time?

4. How does the hen react if the eggs are eaten by a jay or other predator? Does she lay any more?

5. What does she do if the whole nest is destroyed?

6. When does the hen begin to incubate? Is it after the first egg has been laid or after the clutch is complete?

7. How long is the incubation period?

8. Do weather conditions affect the length of the incubation period?

9. Do both cock and hen share the incubation?

10. Which bird incubates at night?

11. Does the cock feed the hen while she is incubating?

12. What happens when the birds change over at the nest? Is there any form of ritual?

13. Do the adults try to decoy intruders away from the nest?

14. Does the hen indicate by her behaviour that the eggs are about to hatch?

15. Do birds recognize their own eggs?

You may ask how it is possible to find the answers to all these questions without disturbing the birds too much. There is a danger that you will make a regular path to the nest and thus reveal its presence to predators; there is also the risk of alarming the parent birds by coming on them too suddenly and causing them to desert. The answer is that you must take every precaution to cover up your tracks and to push protective foliage back into place when you leave the nest.

However strong the temptation, do not visit a nest more often than once a day, and only then if the birds do not seem to be alarmed. Try never to make a bird leave its nest if it is sitting on eggs.

Birds are creatures of habit and you will find that, even when incubation takes place, there are moments when it is possible to find the nest unattended. Some birds become accustomed to visits from humans, particularly if the humans follow a regular routine. For instance, if you make your inspection at the same time each day, approaching the nest from the same direction and generally giving warning of your approach, it is likely that the parent bird will slip off the nest before you are too near; if you depart with the same ostentatious routine, it will get used to slipping back to the nest as soon as you have gone. Birds in nestboxes will

The great crested grebe at its nest, built on decayed water weed

robins, you will notice that the hen leaves the nest for very short periods each day and her mate comes to offer her food on the ground. They do this not very far from the nest but it is possible to check the number of eggs during this brief absence of the hen.

Some of the larger birds moult during the incubation period. Sparrow-hawks, for instance, moult their wing and tail feathers at the same time that they incubate and, if you know of a nest, you can collect the feathers from the ground below. Visit the area regularly and you may find that you have sufficient feathers to mount on a card as a reconstructed wing or tail. If you record the date on which you find each feather, you should be able to determine the length of time the moult lasts. In any case, you will learn a lot about feathers and become practised at distinguishing between primaries, secondaries and so on.

By keeping watch on nests of different species you soon learn that there are different answers to all the questions listed on previous pages. This is one of the reasons why bird-watching is never boring. There may be moments of waiting and even of disappointment when the bird you are watching for does not appear, but these moments are soon forgotten when you eventually find the answer.

As soon as the young are hatched

sometimes become so accustomed to inspection that they do not bother to leave the nest until you are really close.

In many species the cock feeds the hen while she is incubating. If you get the chance to watch a pair of the garden seems suddenly full of adult birds flying to and fro, gathering food for their ever hungry youngsters. It is at this time that you will probably see nest sanitation taking place. Not all young birds stay in the nest after they have hatched. Many waterfowl, for instance, leave the nest quite soon, and ducklings hatched in the morning can often swim by evening. Partridges and lapwings sometimes run off almost as soon as they are out of the egg. Birds which belong to this group are called *nidifugous*; they are born with their eyes open and have at least a covering of down. By contrast, *nidicolous* birds are born naked, with their eyes closed and they remain in the nest until they are able to fly.

The table below gives the duration of the incubation period and the time that is spent in the nest after hatching:

NIDIFUGOUS BIRDS

Species	Incubation Period (Days)
Mute swan	35–36
Grey lag goose	28–29
Mallard	28
Great crested grebe	28
Lapwing	24
Little ringed plover	24–26
Curlew	28–30
Black-tailed godwit	22–24
Herring gull	25–27
Coot	21–24
Common partridge	24–25
Quail	16–21

A kittiwake sheltering her young on a cliff

87

FIGURE 46 *The hoopoe: a scarce but regular migrant to Britain*

NIDICOLOUS BIRDS

Species	Incubation (Days)	Time Spent in Nest (Days)
Jay	16–17	19–20
Starling	14	21
Chaffinch	12–13	13–14
Yellowhammer	12–14	12–14
Skylark	11	9
Great tit	13–14	15–20
Red-backed shrike	14–15	12–15
Spotted flycatcher	12–13	13–14
Song-thrush	13–14	13–15
Sedge warbler	13–14	13–14
Blackbird	13–14	13–15
Redstart	13–14	12–14
Wren	14–16	15–17
Swallow	14–16	20–22
Great spotted woodpecker	15–17	19–21
Swift	18–20	35–56
Hoopoe	16–19	24–27
Kingfisher	21	23–26
Tawny owl	28–30	28–35
Cuckoo	12–13	21–23
Kestrel	29	27–33
Peregrine	28–31	35–40
Buzzard	34–38	42–49
Sparrow-hawk	31–33	26–29
Heron	25–26	50–55
Wood-pigeon	15–17	21–28

Watching events at the nest consumes so much time that in your first season you will not be able to make observations on more than a few species. It is tempting to try to keep track of several nests, but you are bound to miss important data if you watch too many at once. Try to find the answers to the following questions for at least one species:

1. How many of the first clutch of eggs actually hatch?
2. How many times do the adults carry food to the nest in a given period (e.g. one hour)?
3. Do the adults follow a fixed route when approaching the nest with food? Do they ever visit the nest for any other purpose?
4. Is the inside of the throat (gape) marked in a conspicuous way?
5. What colour is the naked nestling? What changes in colour take place as it grows older?
6. After how many days do the eyes open?
7. What induces the young to open their beaks? Is it the presence of their parents? Do they respond to noises, or to anyone touching the nest?
8. At what time of day do they leave the nest for the first time?

9. How far away do they move on the first day? Do they return to the nest? Do they move outside the parents' territory?

10. How do they make their whereabouts known to their parents?

11. Do they approach birds of different species and beg for food?

12. Do the adults build another nest and raise a second brood?

Consideration and patience

There is one golden rule for bird-watchers and this is of vital importance during the breeding season: your first consideration should always be the birds. No matter how much you want to find out about them, all your efforts will be in vain unless you leave them free to behave naturally. It is a complete waste of time to watch a nest full of eggs while the parent birds fly restlessly in the vicinity, too terrified to approach because of your nearness to the nest. The considerate and patient watcher is the one who will be successful.

One day you may be lucky enough to come across a nest in which a cuckoo has laid her egg. Cuckoo eggs have been found in the nests of

A sparrow-hawk at the nest

A young plover. Its colouring blends with the surroundings

more than 50 different species. In Britain they are often found in the nests of hedge-sparrows, robins, meadow-pipits and warblers of various species. Cuckoo eggs vary in size and colour and they are usually just a little larger than those of the foster parent, with the colour matching pretty well. When the cuckoo lays her egg she removes one or two eggs from the nest. The young cuckoo is

FIGURE 47 *Imagine how frightened you would feel if an enormous bird suddenly peered down at you like this*

90

A hedge-sparrow feeding a young cuckoo. Her plumage is frayed and bedraggled as a result of the strain of bringing up the cuckoo

Kittiwakes and guillemots on a Farne Islands cliff-face

no less cunning and, soon after hatching, it begins its destructive work in the nest. With its broad back it pushes out eggs and nestlings alike until it is on its own in the nest. It constantly begs for food and within a few days it doubles its size. As a young cuckoo eats as much as five or six other nestlings, the unfortunate foster parents have their work cut out to keep the young cuckoo satisfied. It leaves the nest after about three weeks and is then fed, outside the nest, for a further two weeks or so.

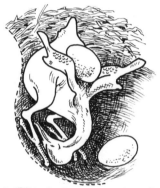

FIGURE 48 *This is how a young cuckoo evicts eggs and nestlings from the nest*

It is thought that cuckoos usually lay their eggs in nests belonging to the same species by which they (the parent cuckoos) were reared.

Bearing in mind the size of an adult cuckoo and the size of nest in which it lays its egg, it is obviously a difficult task to deliver the egg safely in the nest. Should you ever have the luck to observe a cuckoo laying her egg, be sure to write down exactly what you see and watch the process

A sedge warbler acts as foster parent to a young cuckoo

from start to finish. In fact detailed observations at the nest for all species are well worth making.

93

Herons

White stork

Black-headed gull

Herring gull

Buzzard

Black tern

Osprey

Common tern

Lapwing

Coot

Moorhen

W. Söltner

Bean geese

Pintail

Mallards

Shoveler

Reed warbler

Great crested grebe

Tufted duck

Teal

W. Söllner

FIGURE 49 *These birds can be seen in parts of Britain either in summer or autumn, except for bean geese which arrive in winter. The white stork is an uncommon passage bird*

CHAPTER TEN

Taking Care of Birds

Giving first-aid · *Convalescence* · *Rehabilitation*

O N YOUR WALKS and expeditions you are almost certain to find the odd fledgling which appears to have fallen from the nest or been deserted. Your first reaction is to pick up the young bird and, if you cannot find the nest, to take it home and try to look after it. Although this is understandable, it is not necessarily desirable from the point of view of the fledgling. Adult birds keep a sharp eye on their young brood and are often in the neighbourhood, waiting for humans to move on, before going to the assistance of the fledgling which appears to have been deserted.

Should there be any immediate danger to the fledgling, such as from cats, traffic, etc., it is best to pick up the bird and put it in a safe place as near to the original spot as possible. A few branches tied together will make an improvised "cradle" and the young bird can safely be placed in this; should it appear restless, it is worth covering it with a handkerchief for a few minutes as this calms the bird down. It can then be left alone, and the parent birds will probably find it quickly when they return. Unlike some other animals, birds do not desert their young after they have been handled by humans.

Some fledglings leave the nest at a very early age. Young owls, for example, are rather adventurous and soon climb about the branches near the nest; naturally, they sometimes get too ambitious and take a tumble. They immediately make a great fuss, calling attention to their plight, and the casual passer-by assumes the worst. If he wants to be helpful, he will not take the young owl home but will put it on a branch close to the tree trunk.

Giving first aid

Finding an injured bird—as distinct from one which appears to be abandoned—is a different matter altogether. You may well feel an immediate desire to pick the bird up and take it home, where you will try to nurse it back to health. This is a very natural reaction to the sight of any injured animal, but it is important to remember that it is hard work looking after sick creatures, particularly birds, which need frequent feeding. It is no good taking on the job if your enthusiasm is not going to last as long as it takes the bird to get well.

It is also important to realise that birds cannot survive accidents as well as we usually can. When a bird breaks a wing it has very little chance of survival in the wild. It cannot hunt properly for food, nor can it fly away from its enemies. It probably cannot find a warm, dry place to roost.

If you find a bird that is so badly injured that it is unlikely to recover, or if you are not certain that you can look after it properly, then it is better to face up to the situation and put the creature out of its misery. If a wild bird allows you to pick it up, it is

The author found this avocet's nest which was threatened by rising water

97

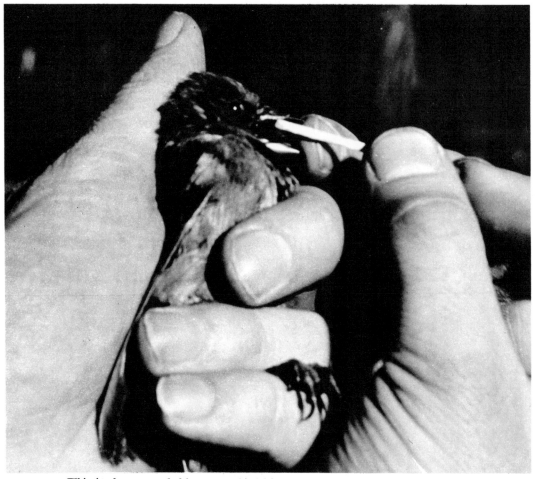

This is the way to hold a young bird if you have to encourage it to take food

probably not going to live much longer. However, occasionally a bird flies into a wire and the impact knocks it unconscious. It should then be kept quiet in a warm, dark place for a few hours, for example in a closed but ventilated box or hanging in a tightly tied bag from which it cannot escape. Often birds recover from the shock quite quickly and are fit to release after a period of rest.

Another disaster that can happen to birds, particularly to those that live in water, is to get oil on their plumage. Seabirds, especially razorbills and guillemots, swim into patches of oil discharged from ships, and river birds such as mute swans sometimes become badly fouled for the same reason. A bird with oiled plumage is a sorry sight; it can no longer fly properly and, unless help is given, the bird will gradually lose condition and die. If you find an oiled bird you should at once tell the local branch of the Royal Society for the Prevention of Cruelty to Animals. Tending oiled birds is a job for experts, who use special equipment for cleaning and feeding them.

Transporting an injured bird may be done in several ways. For small birds a cardboard box is ideal, providing the box is not too large. The smaller the box the quieter the bird will be as it will have little room to move about, and this is important in the case of a sick bird. If it only has to be transported for a short time it can be carried in a paper bag or even wrapped in a handkerchief.

To prevent a bird of prey from damaging its wings, it should be put into a long, footless sock; the bird's head remains free and its legs are bound together with soft material. The sock should fit closely so that the bird cannot flutter its wings and run the risk of damaging its feathers. Caution must be exercised in holding birds with long beaks, such as herons, gannets, etc., as their beaks are a formidable weapon and a moment's carelessness may mean the loss of an eye. Talons should also be treated with respect as these can cause flesh wounds. If a bird is scrabbling with its feet, give it a small stick to hold.

External wounds, such as are made by the pellets of an airgun, can be treated if they are only superficial. If the bleeding can be stopped, the treatment should be the same as for any other wound. It should be cleaned with soap and water, but do not use a detergent. Apply a little antiseptic ointment and bandage if necessary.

Internal injuries and broken bones are cases for a veterinary surgeon. There is often little that can be done. If it is obvious that the bird is suffering, it should be quickly and painlessly destroyed. If you can bear to do this yourself, you should give the bird a hard blow on the back of its head.

Convalescence

Once first aid has been given the question of housing and feeding the patient arises. The more natural food that can be supplied the better. Drinking water must also be provided. Insect-eaters, such as robins, blackbirds and hedge-sparrows, can be fed on small worms, insects and beetles. These are not always easy to find, and you can instead feed the birds on a special mixture supplied by pet shops for insect-eating birds. Tiny helpings of tinned dog-meat and yolk from hard-boiled eggs are also suitable, but do not offer fish. Short, thin strips of meat are only all right if they are accompanied by a special vitamin preparation.

FIGURE 50 *The bullfinch*

Seed-eaters, such as finches and sparrows, prefer grain and seeds which contain a lot of fat, such as sunflower, peanuts and beech nuts. Suitable seeds and nuts can easily be obtained from a pet shop. Fledglings are best fed on a varied diet of soft food; this too can often be bought ready mixed from a pet shop. Small baby birds can in addition be given mealworms, together with dampened white bread to balance their diet. Larger fledglings can eat small pieces of yolk from hard-boiled eggs and soaked pieces of crushed biscuit.

Feeding must take place at regular intervals. It is wrong to feed every few minutes when one happens to have some spare time and then to neglect the bird for several hours. A routine of $1\frac{1}{2}$ to 2 hours should be established. If an extra meal is given last thing at night, it should not be necessary to feed again until the following morning. It is essential that the bird is kept in a room at an even temperature, not too warm, and away from draughts. A budgerigar cage makes a good "hospital" for a small sick bird. It should not be disturbed more than is necessary.

There may be times when a bird refuses to take the food offered and hand feeding may be necessary. This can prove a difficult task and it requires patience and skill. Hold the bird in the left hand with its head resting between your thumb and forefinger; hold the legs gently between the middle and fourth fingers. A little food is picked up on a matchstick, dipped into water, and then pushed behind the bird's tongue. In most cases the beak will open automatically but if the bird does not react in this way, the following method should be used: open the beak gently with your fingers and hold it apart with thumb and forefinger, then push the food as far down the bird's throat as you can manage. Offer only a little food at a

FIGURE 51 *The partridge*

An eagle owl

time and do not hurry the bird. The smaller the bird the more difficult it will be to feed. Owls and other birds of prey should be fed on red meat. When they show signs of getting better add some roughage, such as hair or feathers, to their diet.

One word of caution about handling sick and injured birds. Like people, birds are liable to catch a number of diseases, and some of these can affect human beings. You should therefore always wash your hands after touching birds. It is also a good thing to keep wild birds away from any pet ones that you might have in your home.

Rehabilitation

To be able to release a bird which you have nursed back to health is a wonderful reward. Adult birds can often be set free as soon as they are fit because they are able to resume their normal way of life at once, but if your patient came to you as a young bird, this can present a real problem. It has to learn how to forage for itself and not wait for food to be offered by a human. Insect- and grain-eaters should be given their food on the ground and as much natural food as possible should be offered. Live insects should be given, for instance, or the bird will not recognize its food in the wild.

Young birds of prey and owls have to learn that their food actually moves across the ground at speed. In the wild the young learn to hunt by following the example of their parents, but when the young have been reared by human hands they have no one to teach them how to catch their prey in the wild. The important thing is to teach them that their food moves: this can be done by putting the bird in an empty room and allowing it to get hungry, food is then tied to a piece of string and drawn across the floor, slowly at first but with the speed increasing each day. The bird gradually realizes that it has to grab its food while on the move and in this way it learns to hunt.

After it has been released, a bird

FIGURE 52 *Moorhens taking off*

might take a little time to learn to find its own meals, and it is best to put out some food for the first few days. If this food is not taken for two or three days running, then you can be sure that the bird no longer depends on your help.

You are more likely to find injured birds than dead ones on your expeditions. Nothing goes to waste in Nature; as soon as a bird dies there are many creatures waiting to dispose of it. An extra meal is always welcome to crows, magpies and jays, hedgehogs and so on. A sexton beetle may work the small corpse under ground for its own use. In this way everything is cleared up in the animal world. It is not natural, therefore, to come across a number of dead birds in one district; if this does arise, careful observations should be made of any signs which may give clues as to the cause of death. Insecticides or poisons may have been put down. For instance, it has been proved that owls have died after eating rodents which, although still alive, had a slow-acting poison in their bodies. Whilst an insecticide may not be directly harmful to a bird, it will certainly deprive birds of their natural food supply in the long run.

Birds, like other wild animals, are facing new threats every year from

FIGURE 54 *The capercaillie*

man's activities. Sometimes numbers of birds suddenly die as a result of an accident involving oil, for example, or agricultural chemicals. It is important to let nature conservationists know of any such accident, not only because birds are suffering but also because there might be a risk of man being affected too. If you come across a number of dead or dying birds, make a note of the number and species involved, the place and any other relevant details, and send this information promptly to The Research Department, The Royal Society for the Protection of Birds, The Lodge, Sandy, Bedfordshire SG19 2DL.

FIGURE 53 *Herons*

103

Knots (Calidris canutus) *over the Middle Eye, Cheshire Dee*

CHAPTER ELEVEN

Bird Migration

Height and distance · Using the sun
to find the way · The migratory instinct
Where to see migration · Bird ringing

SCARCELY HAS MAN fulfilled his ancient dream of flying like the birds than he has conquered the sound barrier and gone to the moon. Scientific knowledge continues to advance at an astonishing speed, but often it takes many years to overcome technical difficulties in applying this knowledge.

When you look at the intricate dials and precision instruments in the cockpit of a modern aircraft, you cannot but admire the skill with which Man has perfected his technique for controlling mechanical flight. A bird can accomplish all that an aircraft can do; when you look at its small body, your admiration inevitably turns to wonder.

Height and distance

Not only can birds fly but some are capable of climbing to a great height and of flying over vast distances of strange ocean in non-stop flight. Many Arctic terns breed north of the Arctic Circle, and travel in autumn to the Antarctic, where they stay until March. They thus fly almost from one end of the world to the other twice a year. Migrants return to their breeding-grounds year after year and often build their nests in the same site as in the previous year. Let us now consider the way in which a bird finds its way—orientates—and look at some of the experiments which have been devised to study this.

Using the sun to find the way

In 1950 the late Dr. Gustav Kramer of the Max Planck-Institute in Wilhelmshaven, Germany, developed a series of experiments to test the orientation abilities of birds. His experiments were an impressive example of how one can use a hobby to enrich scientific knowledge. When the time came for his tame starlings to migrate, Dr. Kramer noticed that they fluttered against the side of their cage even to the extent of battering themselves. He noticed that they always fluttered against the cage bars in a certain direction.

To make sure that he was right, he put a starling in a round cage and placed it on a table in a round, empty tower with windows on all sides. He was able to lie on his back under the table and watch the starling without the bird being aware of his presence. He saw that the starling always tried to fly away in the same direction as long as the sun was shining but as soon as it was obscured by cloud, the starling became unsettled and fluttered aimlessly in all directions against the cage. This made him wonder if it orientated by the sun.

During the course of the day the sun's position naturally changed: in the morning it rose in the east and at noon it was high in the sky, yet the bird still flew in the same direction. If the bird really was influenced by the sun, it must have some mechanism which made allowance for movements of the sun and the time of day. To prove this, Dr. Kramer decided to "mislead" the starling. He fixed large mirrors on the outside of the tower windows and was thus able to deflect the sun's rays. For example, he altered their direction by 180 degrees with the result that the starling also altered its flight direction by 180 degrees.

To make quite certain, he tested the starling in other ways. He mounted twelve small food containers around the bird's cage but only one of the containers held any food. This one was placed exactly in the east at sunrise and although the bird could not distinguish between the empty and full containers, it soon learned to find the one with food in it. The food was next put out in

FIGURE 55 *Starlings. They orientate by the sun*

the same place at noon, instead of in the early morning, when the sun was no longer in the east. Nevertheless, the bird flew to the right place without hesitation; this showed that it was able to fly in the same direction (in this case due east) not only when the sun happened to be there but also at other times. It must, therefore, be able to make allowance for the position of the sun according to the time of day.

Dr. Kramer then repeated these experiments, out of sight of the real sun, using a kind of searchlight as an

106

Starlings settling to roost

artificial sun. He was able to imitate the movements of the real sun with his artificial sun, and he found that the starling in its cage was completely "taken in" and orientated itself by the dummy sun. He even made his "sun" rise at midnight and set six hours too early, after following a normal course from east to west, and again the starling was "fooled". However, by shifting the time of the "sun's" movements by six hours—a quarter of a day—he caused the starling to shift its direction by a quarter of the sun's arc (in other words: 90 degrees) and it looked for its food container in the north instead of in the east. It therefore seemed proved that migrating starlings, and probably other day migrants, orientate themselves by the sun's position in its arc, relative to their movements and according to the time of day.

Not all birds migrate by day; the next question which needed answering concerned the birds which migrate at night. This time the Swiss scientists, F. and E. Sauer, carried out similar experiments with night migrants—various warblers—and instead of the artificial sun, they used the revolving starry "sky" of a planetarium. As a result they found that the warblers orientated themselves by the position of the stars. These experiments of Dr. Kramer and the Sauers have been followed up independently by other ornithologists, such as Professor G. V. T. Matthews, who is the Scientific Director of the Wildfowl Trust in Britain.

The migratory instinct

Birds migrate under the influence of climatic conditions, but how do they know when the weather is going to become either warmer or colder? As climatic changes are closely related to the shortening or lengthening of daylight, it is reasonable to assume that light conditions influence the birds' behaviour. Daylight stimulates certain glands in the bird's brain: it becomes restless and sets out on its journey. When experimental birds were injected (outside the migration season) with hormones similar to those produced in their own bodies, they developed the same signs of restlessness and began to try to migrate. The activity rhythm of these glands explains why migrant birds leave our latitudes in the autumn even though food is still abundant. How else could birds know that the time of food scarcity will come in a few months?

You cannot fail to have noticed that many species arrive in the spring and depart in the autumn; some even arrive in late autumn and spend the winter with us. There are other species which appear to stay with us all the time and are true residents. There are *full migrants* like the golden oriole, the swallow, the stork and the cuckoo—all these are very regular in their comings and goings in various countries.

Then there are species which wander within certain areas and their movements are largely determined by

A winter visitor—the fieldfare

108

the weather—these are the *partial migrants*. A whole range of species, such as the starling, behave like migrants in some regions and like residents in others. For instance some blackbirds and buzzards, which are normally residents, have been known to migrate while their brothers and sisters, from the same nest, remain at home. For these reasons, the migration data given in this book should only be used as a general guide.

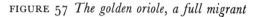

FIGURE 57 *The golden oriole, a full migrant*

FIGURE 56 *Hirundines: full migrants.* Left: *house martin.* Right: *swallow.* Below: *sand martin*

Exceptions occur from time to time and records of any apparently unusual behaviour of this kind are always worth keeping. As it is often difficult to be sure whether the birds seen are residents or on passage, the following general definitions may help:

1. Residents (species which are present all the year round).
2. Summer residents (species which stay for the breeding season only).
3. Winter visitors (species which stay for the winter only).

Factors which influence bird movements

In some years species which are normally resident leave their breeding-grounds in large numbers and invade regions where they are not normally seen. Such irruptions are usually caused by the failure of food supplies in the birds' normal habitat or by abnormal weather conditions, and sometimes by a combination of these two factors. Species such as waxwings and crossbills irrupt from time to

FIGURE 58 *A black stork*

109

time from their main breeding-grounds in north-eastern Europe, and this gives bird-watchers in Britain a chance to see these comparatively uncommon species. On the Continent nutcrackers and Pallas's sandgrouse are also given to irruption. In some cases the irruptions act as a kind of natural safety valve when over-population occurs in the breeding areas. Sometimes a sudden abundance of food in certain areas attracts large numbers of birds from other areas; a plague of voles and other rodents, for instance, may attract short-eared owls and other birds of prey.

From time to time birds are driven from their normal haunts by strong winds and bad weather. Birds driven in this way are not regarded as "invaders" and are usually coastal or sea birds, such as gannets, auks and so on. An interesting case of the powerful effect of weather on birds occurred during December, 1927. A flock of 500 to 1,000 lapwings was carried by strong winds from Britain to Newfoundland, a distance of some 2,000 miles, within twenty-four hours. The lapwings must have travelled, therefore, at an approximate speed of 80 m.p.h.

When observing migrating birds, one should always make allowance for weather conditions. Sudden changes

A puffin with its beak full of fish. Sometimes these birds are driven off course by bad weather

FIGURE 59 *The gannet. These birds can be driven away from home by bad weather*

can hasten the departure of birds in autumn and winter. Cold, icy winds can make the bird-watcher despair of ever seeing another bird, while in clear, sunny weather whole flocks fly at such heights that they become temporarily invisible. Strong winds, as well as complete calm, can bring migration to a halt; weak or moderate winds, on the other hand, are favourable to migrants.

Where to see bird migration

Where can you see migration at its best? There are a few species which migrate on a narrow front, such as cranes, white storks, red-backed shrikes, turnstones, avocets, arctic and sandwich terns. If one happens to be along the route followed by birds such as cranes or white storks, migration is an impressive sight. In the marshes of

northern Germany, for instance, as many as 10,000 cranes have been known to gather in the autumn to start their long journey across France to south-west Spain. The routes taken by white storks, when travelling from Europe to South Africa are shown in Figure 60; as the storks belong to the "gliders", they avoid crossing over large stretches of water and prefer to fly over land, although this means a longer journey.

Most species migrate on a broad front and are, therefore, more difficult

FIGURE 60 *An example of recorded migration: storks migrate to the south by two routes— westward over Spain and eastward over Turkey, Israel and Egypt*

FIGURE 60a *Migrating storks*

to observe. They are often concentrated into an aerial stream by such natural barriers as ranges of hills and mountains or along rivers and coastlines. The best places to watch such movements are on the coast, from promontories, along island chains, mountain passes and rivers.

Coastal migration is often the most easily observed in Britain and you will find September and October the best months for expeditions of this kind. Figure 63 shows the main routes followed by day migrants in autumn over the British Isles. From this map you can easily decide which places are best for watching. Lighthouses are well worth visiting because night migrants are often glimpsed in the beams from the lantern, and the following morning there are frequently tired migrants to be seen, resting in the lighthouse garden. Night travellers such as warblers and thrushes may come down for a rest

before continuing their journey. Lighthouse keepers often take an interest in birds, and they may be able to offer you local information.

If you are a newcomer to migration watching, it is well worth paying a visit to one of the bird observatories because you will then have the benefit of guidance from experienced ornithologists. Observatories along the east coast, such as Spurn, Gibraltar Point and Dungeness, are excellent for watching migration and they are much more accessible than some of the island observatories.

FIGURE 61 *The crane. These birds gather in large numbers in northern Europe for migration*

A migrant—the arctic tern

Migration may also be seen inland and even over large cities. London bird-watchers have shown convincingly that it is not necessary to go to the coast to watch birds migrating. Local hills, river valleys and sewage farms may prove to be good places— sewage provides a rich source of food

113

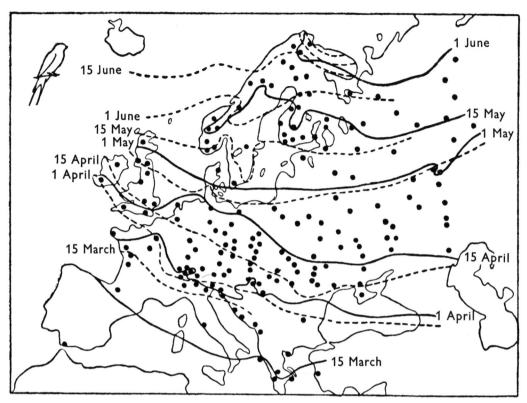

FIGURE 62 *Spring arrival dates of the swallow in Europe The black lines show the progress of swallows in various parts of Europe by the date shown on the right-hand side of the map. The dotted lines link all the places with a temperature of 8.9 degrees Centigrade (48 degrees Fahrenheit). Notice that, up to 1st May, swallows are arriving behind the 8.9 degrees isotherm but after that date they are in advance of it*

for tired migrants—and you may well discover unsuspected routes in your own locality. The study of migration inland has been rather neglected and more information is needed on this. Although autumn movements of birds are the easiest to observe, spring migration should not be ignored and, as the routes taken by migrants in spring are not always the same as those taken in the autumn, interesting comparisons can be made.

Bird-watching in the migrating season is full of interest. The fact that birds migrate enables us to see species which do not nest in our own country and the migration season is the most promising time for observing rare birds. Quite apart from this, the movements of birds are a fascinating study. The charts given in the Appendix refer to "normal" breeding dates and migration dates, but slight variations occur in these dates due

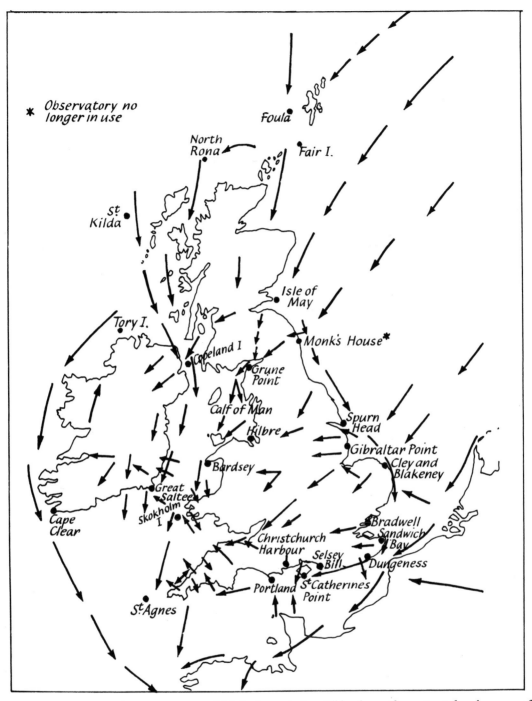

FIGURE 63 *Autumn bird movements and bird observatories. This shows the routes taken by some of the song birds, waders and wildfowl which invade the British Isles in the autumn. (Watch points which have not yet been granted observatory status are also included)*

FIGURE 64 *The ruff*

2. Dates of departure. When does the movement reach its peak?
3. Is the date influenced by local weather conditions (temperature, wind, cloudy or clear sky)?
4. What effect, if any, does food supply have?

to local weather conditions and geographical position. Interesting comparisons can be made from year to year and, as weather can affect migration, it is important to be familiar with weather forecasts and to keep detailed notes of weather conditions.

If you wish to study bird migration closely, it is well worth making your own charts and time-tables on which to record the movements you observe. There are a number of points which you should look out for and make notes on:

1. Who begins the journey, the adults or the young, males or females?

Migratory birds sometimes pause for a while in a district before resuming their travels, and your charts should show when these passage migrants arrive and how long they stay. Here, too, weather conditions should be recorded, and if an unusual species "invades" the district, try to discover the reason. It is also useful to record how long the invasion lasts.

Studying migration

A great advance in the practical study of migration took place in 1890 when a Danish schoolmaster, Hans Christian Mortensen, first put small tin rings, stamped with a serial number and address, round the legs of birds. Later, ornithologists began to use aluminium rings, which are easier to handle and which do not corrode. Bird-ringing in Britain started seriously in 1909, largely on the initiative of the late H. F. Witherby, and it was run under the auspices of the magazine *British Birds*.

FIGURE 65 *The storm petrel*

116

The sand martin with brown upper-parts and white under-parts

Nowadays the ringing scheme is organized and administered by the British Trust for Ornithology.

Bird ringing

There are many bird observatories, ringing stations and ringing schemes all over the world and large numbers of individual ringers take part in this work. Birds are ringed as nestlings or are trapped regularly each year and ringed. Details of the birds' weight and physical condition are recorded carefully. The list of ringed birds now runs into millions of individuals of many species.

Bird ringing is carried out only by qualified people, and anyone taking part in this work must possess sufficient knowledge to be capable of working to a strict ethical and practical code. If you wish to become a ringer in Britain, you must have reached the age of fourteen before you can start to train. You must study with qualified ringers before you can apply for a permit to catch and ring birds on your own. For additional experience you might like to visit one or more bird observatories. Here you will be able to see large permanent Heligoland traps, named after the German observatory where they were invented. You might also be lucky enough to see species that do not occur near your home, especially migrants.

It cannot be guaranteed that the warden or other experienced ringers will have sufficient time to teach you all these things, but at least you can watch how it is done and, when the opportunity arises for you to gain some experience under expert tuition, you will then be in a position to ask for the necessary recommendation. Full details of entry into the ringing scheme can be obtained from the Ringing and Migration Office, British Trust for Ornithology, Beech Grove, Tring, Hertfordshire HP23 5NR.

Whether you become a ringer or not, you should at least try to make yourself familiar with the various types of rings in use so that you know whom to inform when you find one. The rings issued by the B.T.O. vary in size and strength according to the size of bird for which they have been designed. Rings from foreign stations look rather similar.

If a ring is completely closed—looking solid all the way round—you can be certain that it has come from a caged bird of some kind. Many rings found by ordinary people are those put on pigeons by pigeon fanciers. These rings usually carry a combination of letters and a number (e.g., NURP 6830) and should be sent to the National Homing Union, 22 Clarence Street, Gloucester, and *not* to the B.T.O.

If you find a genuine wild bird ring, either foreign or British, you should send it immediately to the Secretary of the B.T.O. Bird Ringing Committee. The following information should be sent with the ring:

1. The species to which the ring was attached, if possible (you may be able to identify the corpse of the bird).

Everyone who co-operates in the ringing scheme, either as a ringer or finder, helps to build up our knowledge of the way ·in which birds live. Recoveries of ringed birds or of rings from dead birds may provide valuable information about the routes taken on migration, the longevity of birds, for how long they pair, whether

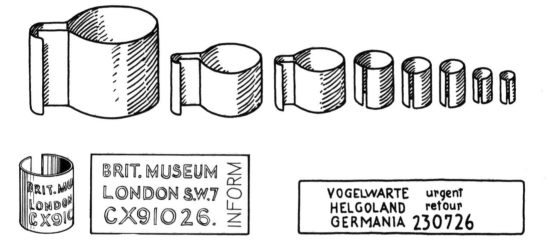

FIGURE 66 *An example of some British and foreign bird rings*

2. The exact locality where the ring was found and the precise circumstances under which it was found (e.g. whether the bird was shot, had flown into telegraph wires, was killed by a predatory animal).
3. The address of the finder.

In due course the finder will receive a report giving details of where the bird was originally ringed.

they return to the same breeding-site each year and so on.

Field observations of any kind which are faithfully recorded on the spot will not only give you a lasting record of your experiences with birds but they may also be of interest to professional ornithologists. By studying books and reading bird magazines, you will gradually learn more about birds, and all this will give you many hours of both interest and excitement.

Bird-watchers never seem to find life boring, and the more they know about birds the more they want to find out about the many aspects of bird life which are still not fully understood.

Shags on the Farne Islands

Appendix

Societies of Interest to Bird-watchers

Royal Society for the Protection of Birds, The Lodge, Sandy, Bedfordshire SG19 2DL.
   The Society manages more than 40 bird reserves. To visit most of these permits must be obtained from the RSPB. For young people up to the age of 18 there is a junior section called the Young Ornithologists' Club, which organises projects, outings and courses, and has a quarterly magazine.

British Trust for Ornithology, Beech Grove, Tring, Hertfordshire HP23 5NR.
   Individual research and permanent studies, such as a national bird ringing scheme, a common bird census and a nest records scheme, are organised. The Trust publishes a quarterly journal and a regular bulletin. Membership is half-price for people aged under 21.

Wildfowl Trust, Slimbridge, Gloucestershire GL2 7BT.
   The Trust maintains collections of the world's ducks, geese and swans, and a number of refuges for wild birds; all these are open to the public. Young people up to the age of 18 may become Gosling members of the Trust and are entitled to free access to the Trust's refuges and a quarterly bulletin. A Gosling party is held every Christmas. There are various wildfowl identification tests by which Goslings are promoted through different grades.

Field Studies Council, 9 Devereux Court, Strand, London WC2R 3JR.
   The Council organises residential courses for young people at field centres. Programmes are issued annually, and there is a warden at each centre from whom detailed information may be obtained. The centres are:

   Dale Fort Field Centre, Haverfordwest, Pembrokeshire.
   The Drapers' Field Centre, Rhyd-y-creuau, Betws-y-coed, Caernarvonshire.
   Flatford Mill Field Centre, East Bergholt, Colchester, Essex CO7 6UL.
   Juniper Hall Field Centre, Dorking, Surrey RH5 6DA.
   The Leonard Wills Field Centre, Nettlecombe Court, Williton, Taunton, Somerset.
   Malham Tarn Field Centre, Settle, Yorkshire BD24 9PU.

Orielton Field Centre, Pembroke, Pembrokeshire.
Preston Montford Field Centre, Montford Bridge, Shrewsbury SY4 1DX.
Slapton Ley Field Centre, Slapton, Kingsbridge, Devon TQ7 2QP.

There are many county and local societies for bird-watchers. Your local public library will have the details. The Royal Society for the Prevention of Cruelty to Animals and the People's Dispensary for Sick Animals will give advice on sick and injured birds. Your library or telephone directory will list the local branches.

Bird Observatories in the British Isles

Bird observatories carry out various forms of research and field-work, including trapping and ringing of migrants. Most of the observatories have accommodation for visitors, but facilities vary and detailed information is available from the British Trust for Ornithology. The main observatories are:

Bardsey Island Bird and Field Observatory, Aberdaron, N. Wales.
Calf of Man Bird Observatory, Isle of Man.
Cape Clear Island Bird Observatory, Co. Cork, Eire.
Copeland Bird Observatory, Co. Down, N. Ireland.
Dungeness Bird Observatory, Romney Marsh, Kent.
Fair Isle Bird Observatory, by Lerwick, Shetland.
Gibraltar Point Bird Observatory, near Skegness, Lincolnshire.
Holme Bird Observatory, Hunstanton, Norfolk.
Isle of May Bird Observatory, Fife.
Jersey Bird Observatory, St Ouen's Bay, Jersey.
Lundy Field Society Observatory, Devon.
Malin Head Bird Observatory, Co. Donegal, Eire.
Mullet Bird Observatory, Co. Mayo, Eire.
Portland Bird Observatory, Portland, Dorset.
Sandwich Bay Bird Observatory, Sandwich, Kent.
Skokholm Island Bird Observatory, Dale, Haverfordwest, Pembrokeshire.
Spurn Bird Observatory, Kilnsea, via Patrington, Hull, Yorkshire.
Tory Island Bird Observatory, Co. Donegal, Eire.
Walney Bird Observatory, Walney Island, Lancashire.

A Short List of Books and Records

The Observer's Book of Birds	S. Vere Benson (Warne)
Birds of the Wayside and Woodland	Enid Blyton (Warne)
Discovering Bird Watching	Jim Flegg (Shire)
Collins' Guide to Bird Watching	R. S. R. Fitter (Collins)
The Bird Table Book	Tony Soper (Pan)

Bird Behaviour	John Sparks (Hamlyn)
The Birds of the British Isles and their Eggs	T. A. Coward (Warne)
The Popular Handbook of British Birds	P. A. D. Hollom (Witherby)
Pocket Guide to British Birds	R. S. R. Fitter and R. A. Richardson (Collins)
A Field Guide to the Birds of Britain and Europe	Roger Peterson, Guy Mountfort, P. A. D. Hollom (Collins)
The Hamlyn Guide to Birds of Britain and Europe	Bertel Bruun and Arthur Singer (Hamlyn)
The Birds of Britain and Europe with North Africa and the Middle East	Hermann Heinzel, R. S. R. Fitter, John Parslow (Collins)
The Young Specialist Looks at Birds	Heinrich Frieling (Burke)
The Shell Bird Book	James Fisher (Ebury Press & Michael Joseph)
Where to Watch Birds	John Gooders (André Deutsch)
Your Book of Photographing Wild Life	John Marchington (Faber)

There are several bird titles in the Ladybird Books series published by Wills & Hepworth.

Sound-Guide to British Birds (Two 12 in. records and a book)	Myles North and Eric Simms (Witherby)
Listen, the Birds (Eighteen 7 in. records)	Hans Traber and John Kirby (European Phono Club)
Bird Sounds in Close-up (12 in.)	Victor C. Lewis (Pye)
Bird Sounds in Close-up, Volume II (12 in.)	Victor C. Lewis (Pye)
Bird Song Adventure (12 in.)	Patrick Sellar and Victor C. Lewis (Pye)
A Year's Journey (12 in.)	Eric Simms (BBC)

Magazines and Pamphlets

Bird Life	Quarterly (R.S.P.B. Young Ornithologists' Club)
Birds	Bi-monthly (R.S.P.B.)
Bird Study	Quarterly (B.T.O.)
World of Birds	Monthly (Grant Demar)
British Birds	Monthly (Witherby)
Nestboxes	J. J. M. Flegg and D. E. Glue (B.T.O.)
Binoculars, Telescopes, Cameras	J. J. M. Flegg (B.T.O.)
A Species List of British and Irish Birds	Robert Hudson (B.T.O.)
Treatment of Sick and Injured Birds	R.S.P.B.
Wild Birds and the Law	R.S.P.B.
Information on Feeding Birds	R.S.P.B.

Residents, Passage Migrants, Summer and Winter Visitors

In the following lists, species are assigned to particular categories:

1. *Residents* (Birds that are usually resident in some part of the British Isles.)

2. *Passage migrants* (Birds that are usually passage migrants, including some species that are now breeding in small numbers.)

3. *Summer and winter visitors* (Birds that are summer residents and non-breeding winter visitors, including species that are sometimes observed out-of-season and some that nest occasionally in the British Isles.)

It should be noted that in many cases a species could be assigned to more than one category; e.g. the woodcock breeds in many parts of the British Isles and it may be seen all the year round but some woodcocks come here only for the summer and depart in the autumn whilst others pass through only in spring and autumn, yet others come here for the winter only; the status of the woodcock could, therefore, be described as resident, summer resident, passage migrant and winter visitor. The assignment of species to these categories is, therefore, somewhat arbitrary but it should serve as a rough guide. Allowances should also be made regarding dates in Table III for geographical variations.

TABLE I RESIDENTS IN SOME PARTS OF THE BRITISH ISLES

Black-throated diver	Wigeon	Hen harrier
Red-throated diver	Pintail	Peregrine
Great crested grebe	Shoveler	Merlin
Slavonian grebe	Mandarin	Kestrel
Black-necked grebe	Tufted duck	Red grouse
Little grebe	Pochard	Ptarmigan
Leach's petrel	Common scoter	Black grouse
Storm petrel	Eider	Capercaillie
Manx shearwater	Red-breasted merganser	Red-legged partridge
Fulmar	Goosander	Partridge
Gannet	Shelduck	Pheasant
Cormorant	Grey lag goose	Water rail
Shag	Canada goose	Moorhen
Heron	Mute swan	Coot
Bittern	Golden eagle	Oyster catcher
Mallard	Buzzard	Lapwing
Teal	Sparrow-hawk	Ringed plover
Gadwall	Kite	Golden plover

Snipe
Woodcock
Curlew
Whimbrel
Black-tailed godwit
Redshank
Greenshank
Dunlin
Avocet
Great black-backed gull
Lesser black-backed gull
Herring gull
Common gull
Black-headed gull
Kittiwake
Razorbill
Guillemot
Black guillemot
Puffin
Stock dove
Rock dove
Wood pigeon
Collared dove
Barn owl
Little owl
Tawny owl
Long-eared owl
Short-eared owl

Kingfisher
Green woodpecker
Great spotted woodpecker
Lesser spotted woodpecker
Wood lark
Sky lark
Raven
Carrion crow
Hooded crow
Rook
Jackdaw
Magpie
Jay
Chough
Great tit
Blue tit
Coal tit
Crested tit
Marsh tit
Willow tit
Long-tailed tit
Bearded tit
Nuthatch
Tree creeper
Wren
Dipper
Mistle thrush
Fieldfare
Song-thrush

Redwing
Blackbird
Stonechat
Robin
Dartford warbler
Goldcrest
Hedge-sparrow
Meadow pipit
Rock pipit
Pied wagtail
Grey wagtail
Starling
Hawfinch
Greenfinch
Goldfinch
Siskin
Linnet
Twite
Redpoll
Bullfinch
Crossbill
Chaffinch
Yellowhammer
Corn bunting
Cirl bunting
Reed bunting
Snow bunting
House-sparrow
Tree sparrow

TABLE II SOME PASSAGE MIGRANTS

(*Denotes species which breed in the British Isles in small numbers)

Sooty shearwater
Velvet scoter
* Osprey
* Quail
Little stint
Curlew sandpiper
* Ruff

Spotted redshank
* Wood sandpiper
Pomarine skua
* Black tern
* Hoopoe
* Wryneck
Richard's pipit

Barred warbler
Yellow-browed warbler
Red-breasted flycatcher
* Firecrest
* Black redstart
Bluethroat
Ortolan bunting

N.B.—Many individuals of other species which are listed in other tables and which breed in other countries, pass through the British Isles on migration and are therefore passage migrants.

TABLE III

Migration Chart of Some Typical Summer and Winter Visitors

SPECIES	STATUS	JAN 1 2 3 4	FEB 1 2 3 4	MAR 1 2 3 4	APR 1 2 3 4	MAY 1 2 3 4	JUN 1 2 3 4	JUL 1 2 3 4	AUG 1 2 3 4	SEP 1 2 3 4	OCT 1 2 3 4	NOV 1 2 3 4	DEC 1 2 3 4
* Great northern diver	wv	w w w w	w w w w	w w w w	w w d d	d d . .	. . . .	. . . .	. . . .	. . . a	a a w w	w w w w	w w w w
Garganey	sv	. . . .	. . . .	. . a a	a a a b	b b b b	b b b b	b b b b	b b b b	d d d d	d d d d	. . . .	. . . .
* Scaup	wv	w w w w	w w w w	w w w w	w w w d	d d d d	d . . .	. . . .	. . . .	. . . a	a a a a	a a w w	w w w w
* Goldeneye	wv	w w w w	w w w w	w w d d	d d d d	d d d .	. . . .	. . . .	. . . .	. . . a	a a a a	a a w w	w w w w
Long-tailed duck	wv	w w w w	w w w w	w w d d	d d d .	d . . .	. . . .	. . . .	. . . .	. . . a	a a a a	w a w w	w w w w
Smew	wv	w w w w	w w w w	w w w d	d d . .	. . . .	. . . .	. . . .	. . . .	. . . .	a a a a	a a a w	w w w w
White-fronted goose	wv	w w w w	w w w w	d d d d	d . . .	. . . .	. . . .	. . . .	. . . .	. . a a	a a a a	w w w w	w w w w
Pink-footed goose	wv	w w w w	w w w w	w w w w	d d d .	. . . .	. . . .	. . . .	. . . .	a a a a	a a a a	w w w w	w w w w
Brent goose	wv	w w w w	w w w w	w w w w	d d d .	. . . .	. . . .	. . . .	. . . .	a a a a	a a a a	w w w w	w w w w
Barnacle goose	wv	w w w w	w w w w	w w w d	d d d .	. . . .	. . . .	. . . .	. . . .	. . a a	a a a a	w w w w	w w w w
* Whooper swan	wv	w w w w	w w w w	w w w d	d d d d	. . . .	. . . .	. . . .	. . . .	. a . .	a a a a	w w w w	w w w w
Bewick's swan	wv	w w w w	w w w w	d d d d	d . . .	. . . .	. . . .	. . . .	. . . .	. . . a	a a a a	w w w w	w w w w
* Marsh harrier	sv	. . . .	. . . .	. . . .	a a a a	a a b b	b b b b	b b b b	b b b b	d d d d	d d d d	. . . .	. . . .
* Montagu's harrier	sv	. . . .	. . . .	. . . .	. a a a	a b b b	b b b b	b b b b	b b b b	d d d d	d d d d	. . . .	. . . .
Hobby	sv	. . . .	. . . .	. . . .	a a a a	b b b b	b b b b	b b b b	b b b b	d d d d	, d d d	. . . .	. . . .
* Corncrake	sv	. . . .	. . . .	. . . .	a a a a	a b b b	b b b b	b b b b	b b b b	a a a a	d d d d	. . . .	. . . .
Little ringed plover	sv	. . . .	. . . .	. . . .	a a a a	a a b b	b b b b	b b b b	b b b b	a a a a	d d d .	. . . .	. . . .
* Grey plover	wv	w w w w	w w w w	w w w d	d d d d	d d d d	. . . .	a a a a	b b b b	a a a a	a a w w	w w w w	w w w w
Dotterel	sv	. . . .	. . . .	. . . .	d d d d	d d a a	a b b b	a a a a	a a a a	d d d d	a a w w	. . . .	. . . .
* Turnstone	wv	w w w w	w w w w	w w d d	d d d d	d d d d	. d . .	a a a a	a a a a	a a a a	a a a w	w w w w	w w w w
Jack snipe	wv	w w w w	w w w w	w w w d	d d d d	. . . .	. . . .	. . . .	. . . .	. . a a	a a a a	a a a w	w w w w
* Bar-tailed godwit	wv	w w w w	w w w w	w w d d	d d d d	d d d d	. . . .	a a a a	a a d d	a a a a	a a a a	w w w w	w w w w
* Green sandpiper	wv	w w w w	w w w w	w w w d	d d d d	d d d b	. . . .	a a b b	b b d d	a a a a	w w w w	w w w w	w w w w
* Common sandpiper	sv	. . . .	. . . .	. . . .	a a a a	a a b b	b b b b	a a a a	d d d d	a a a a	d d . .	. . . .	. . . .
* Knot	wv	w w w w	w w w w	w w w d	d d d d	d . . .	. . . .	. . . .	. . . a	a a a a	a a a w	a a a w	w w w w
* Purple sandpiper	wv	w w w w	w w w w	w w w d	d d d d	d d a a	. . . .	a a a a	b b b b	a a a a	a a a w	w w w w	w w w w
* Sanderling	wv	w w w w	w w w w	w w w d	d d d d	d a a b	. . . .	a a a a	a a a a	a a a a	a a a w	w w w w	w w w w
* Red-necked phalarope	sv	. . . .	. . . .	. . . .	. . . .	a a a a	b b b b	b b b b	b b b b	b b b b	. . . .	. . . .	. . . .
Stone curlew	sv	. . . .	. . . .	. . a a	a a a b	b b b b	b b b b	b b b b	b b b b	b b b b	d d d d	. . . .	. . . .
* Arctic skua	sv	. . . .	. . . .	. . . .	a a a a	a a b b	b b b b	b b b b	b b b b	d d d d	d d d d	. . . .	. . . .

The table spans a yearly calendar divided into monthly/fortnightly columns. I label the data columns 1..24 from left to right (left of the dotted grid is the status column, e.g. sv/wv).

Species	Status	1	2	3	4	5	6	7	8	9	10	11	12	13	14	15	16	17	18	19	20	21	22	23	24
* Great skua	sv									a	a	a	a	b	b	b	b	b	b	b	b	h	b	b	b	d	d	d	d	d	d	d	d				
Little gull	wv	w w w w	w w w w	w w d d	d d d d	d										a a a a	a a a a	a a w w	w w w w	w w w w
Common tern	sv								a a	a a b b	b b b b	b b b b	d d d d	d d d d	d d		
Arctic tern	sv						a	a a a b	b b b b	b b b b	d d d d	d d d d	d d d		
Roseate tern	sv						a a b b	b b b b	b b b b	b d d d	d d		
Little tern	sv						a a a b	b b b b	b b b b	d d d d	d d d d		
Sandwich tern	sv				a	a a a a	b b b b	b b b b	d d d d	d d d d	d d		
Turtle dove	sv				a a	a a b b	b b b b	b b b b	b d d d	d d d d	d		
Cuckoo	sv				a a a a	a a b b	b b b b	b b b d	d d d d	d d		
Nightjar	sv				a	a a b b	b b b b	b b b b	b b b b	d d d d		
Swift	sv				a	a a a b	b b b b	b b b d	d d d d	d		
Shore lark	wv	w w w w	w w w w	w w d d	d d d d										a	a a a a	a a w w	w w w w
Swallow	sv				a a	a a a a	a a b b	b b b b	b b b b	b b b d	d d d d	d d d		
House martin	sv			a a a a	a a a b	b b b b	b b b b	b b b b	b d d d	d d d		
Sand martin	sv			.. b b b	b b b b	b b b b	b b b b	b b d d	d d d d	..		
* Ring ouzel	sv			a a a	a a a b	b b b b	b b b b	b b b b	b b d d	d d d d	d d d d	d	
Wheatear	sv			a a a	a a a b	b b b b	b b b b	b b b d	d d d d	d d d d	d d d		
Whinchat	sv			a	a a a b	b b b b	b b b b	b b b d	d d d d		
Redstart	sv			a a a a	a a b b	b b b b	b b b b	b b b d	d d d d	d	
Nightingale	sv			a a a	a b b b	b b b b	b b b d	d d d d	d d d		
Grasshopper warbler	sv			a a	a a a b	b b b b	b b b b	b d d d	d d d d		
Reed warbler	sv			a a	a a a b	b b b b	b b b b	b b b d	d d d d		
Marsh warbler	sv			.... a a	a b b b	b b b b	d d d d	d		
Sedge warbler	sv			a a a	a a b b	b b b b	b b b b	b b d d	d d d d		
* Blackcap	sv			a	a a a a	a a b b	b b b b	b b b b	b b d d	d d d d	d d d d		
Garden warbler	sv			a a a	a a b b	b b b b	b b b b	b d d d	d d d d	d		
Whitethroat	sv			a a a a	a b b b	b b b b	b b b b	b b b d	d d d d	d d d d	d	
Lesser whitethroat	sv			a a a	b b b b	b b b b	b b b b	b d d d	d d d d	d	
Willow warbler	sv			a a	a a a b	b b b b	b b b b	b b b b	b d d d	d d d d		
* Chiffchaff	sv			a a a	a a a b	b b b b	b b b b	b b b b	d d d d	d d d d	d d	
Wood warbler	sv			a a a	a a b b	b b b b	b b b d	d d d d	d		
Spotted flycatcher	sv			a a a	a a b b	b b b b	b b b b	d d d d	d d d d		
Pied flycatcher	sv			a a	a a b b	b b b b	b b b b	d d d d	d d d d		
Tree pipit	sv			a a a a	a a b b	b b b b	b b b b	d d d d	d d d d	d d		
Yellow wagtail	sv			a a a b	b b b b	b b b b	b b b b	b b d d	d d d d		
Great grey shrike	wv	w w w w	w w w w	w d d d	d d											.. a a a	a a w w	w w w w
Red-backed shrike	sv			a	a a a b	b b b b	b b b b	d d d d	d d d d	d		
* Brambling	wv	w w w w	w w w w	d d d d	d d d d	d d									a	a a a a	a a w w	w w w w

Key

a—arrivals; b—breeding; d—departures; w—wintering; sv—summer visitors; wv—winter visitors

* species sometimes observed out of season